POLITICAL PORTRAITS

GENERAL EDITOR
KENNETH O. MORGAN

ÉAMON DE VALERA

OWEN DUDLEY EDWARDS

THE CATHOLIC UNIVERSITY OF AMERICA PRESS
WASHINGTON, D.C.

The Catholic University of America Press, Washington, D.C.

First published in 1987
© Owen Dudley Edwards, 1987

Library of Congress Cataloging-in-Publication Data
Edwards, Owen Dudley
Eamon de Valera/Owen Dudley Edwards
p.   cm. — (Political portraits)
ISBN 0–8132–0665–0   ISBN 0–8132–0666–9 (pbk.)
1. De Valera, Eamonn, 1882–1975.   2. Ireland—Presidents—
Biography.   3. Ireland—Politics and government—1910–1921.
4. Ireland—Politics and government—1922–1949.
I. Title.   II. Series.
DA965.D4E38   1987
941.7082'2'0924—dc19
[B]

Cover design: T. C. Evans Design Graphics

The publishers wish to acknowledge the advice and assistance given by the Design
Department of the Welsh Books Council which is supported by the Welsh Arts Council.

Set by Quality Phototypesetting, Bristol
Printed in Great Britain at The Bath Press, Avon

Contents

We have not asked you to abandon any principle, even informally, but surely you must understand that we can only recognize ourselves for what we are. If this self-recognition be made a reason for the cancellation of the Conference, we regret it, but it seems inconsistent.

I have already had conference with you, and in these conferences and in my written communications I have never ceased to recognize myself for what I was and am.

—Éamon de Valera to David Lloyd George
(telegram), 17 September 1921

EDDIE CORBONE: Give me back my name, Marco! Give me back my name!

—Arthur Miller, *A View from the Bridge*

For my
Father

Editor's Foreword

The aim of this open-ended series of short biographies is to offer personal portraits of several of the decisive figures in the making of British politics over the past two hundred years. It will range over leading practitioners of politics, from Britain and Ireland (and probably the commonwealth/empire as well) who have vitally shaped our public affairs in the nineteenth and twentieth centuries. Its premise, of course, is that people and biographies are vitally important as explanatory keys to the past. Too often, historians tend to see the course of historical change in terms of vague impersonal factors, evolutionary patterns, underlying themes, even that Scylla and Charybdis of historical understanding, 'forces' and 'trends'. The impact of the disciplines of economics, sociology or anthropology is often taken as reinforcing this tendency, and helping to obliterate flesh-and-blood human beings from our map of the past.

Now, no-one would seriously dispute the enrichment of historical studies that has resulted from the stimulus of other disciplines. At the same time, it can hardly be questioned that the role of key individuals, locally and regionally as well as nationally, has been crucial in shaping the rhythms and speed of our political development in the years since the twin impact of industrialization and representative democracy. The growth of our political parties are impossible to visualize without the personal imprint of Gladstone, Disraeli or Keir Hardie. The course of wars, and their consequences, would have been totally different if Lloyd George or Churchill had never lived. Without Parnell or de Valera, modern Ireland would not have emerged in its present form. Even in the

1980s, the dominance of Mrs Thatcher confirms anew the powerful impulses that can be released by the authority or whim of one determined individual.

So there need be no apology for offering a new series of biographies, brief but authoritative, all written by expert scholars, designed for the intelligent general reader as well as for the student or the specialist, as launch-pads for political and historical understanding. Portraits of individuals, naturally, open up wider social, cultural or intellectual themes. They also help to make history fun—vibrant, vivid, accessible. They may also be a means to a deeper understanding of our world. It should always be remembered that Karl Marx himself, whose influence is so frequently taken as eliminating individuals entirely from history in favour of the rise and conflict of social classes, actually took the reverse view himself. 'History', Marx wrote, 'is nothing but the activity of men in pursuit of their ends.' Some of these men—and women—and the ends they pursued, achieved, missed out on, or simply forgot, are illustrated in this series.

In this present work, Owen Dudley Edwards, a distinguished Irish scholar and man of letters, whose pan-Celtic spirit comprehends a Welsh name, a university post in Scotland and several important books on Irish history, sheds a new, often startling, always provocative light on Éamon de Valera, perhaps the founding spirit of modern Ireland. 'Dev' was always seen to be a subtle and complex man, both before and after Lloyd George discovered the fact for himself during their celebrated dialectical jousting in the summer of 1921. The present closure of de Valera's private papers has made him the more impenetrable. But Mr Dudley Edwards's highly original study uncovers new layers of complexity, both in the man and his outlook, especially in his relationship with the Roman Catholic faith and his perspectives on church and state. Born in Brooklyn, educated in Bruree and Blackrock College, de Valera took a leading role in the 1916 Easter rising in Dublin, and fortuitously escaped execution by the British authorities. He became president of Sinn Féin during the Anglo-Irish war, and strongly resisted the Free State Treaty of 1922 which included the partition of the island. However, he later emerged from the wilderness to become Taoiseach, or head of government, in the newly-independent Ireland, returned to power in 1951 and again in 1957, and finally became the venerated president of the Republic from 1959 to 1973. He died in 1975 after seventy years of involvement in the national struggle.

To many, de Valera always seemed an intransigent, perhaps a bigot. However, as Mr Dudley Edwards graphically shows, his relationship with the national movement at key points in Irish history was many-sided and unique. He came to symbolize continuity and revolution, stability and upheaval, at one and the same time. He had many ambivalent features. Even his passionate commitment to the Irish language had its highly individual aspects. He was vitally important as leader and driving force, but above all else as a proud symbol of an unconquerable nation. Mr Dudley Edwards sees in de Valera a priest-king figure who embodied the sufferings of his people and his faith in his own unyielding person. He also shows the crucial significance of his confessional background during his student days, the varied ideological strains that impelled him into Sinn Féin and republicanism, his uneasy relationship with the Irish-American community in the land in which he was born, and with the Catholic hierarchy, no less than with the British government, in the later years of power. De Valera was clearly an outsider in Ireland itself, a mystical logician, a pragmatic extremist, an aloof populist, a serpentine politician of breathtaking straightforwardness and simplicity. Instead of the usual pattern of historic inevitability, Owen Dudley Edwards depicts Dev as an isolated, almost tangential figure, suddenly thrust into centre stage 'from God knows where'. With all his inner contradictions, he imposed himself on modern Ireland and the Anglo-Irish relationship as powerfully as any nationalist leader of the twentieth century. The realities of his career, no less than the legends, are memorably explored by Mr Dudley Edwards in this biography.

KENNETH O. MORGAN
The Queen's College, Oxford

Preface

The peculiarity of this book requires a note of apology at the outset. Éamon de Valera lived for 92 years. During this time, he played a prominent part in public life from 1916 to 1973, two years before his death, and his 33 years before the Easter Rising are clearly of importance in explaining how he came to play the part he did. Instead of providing a year-by-year narrative I have been led to approach the question of his biography in a more analytical fashion. A first chapter offers an interpretation of his particular form of leadership, which I find unusual in the extreme. I have then turned to his beginnings, which are such as to supply some answers to his career. The fact that, to me, so much about him is explained by his very strange background may seem to be at variance with the general historiographical pattern of his life: in part this is because most of his biographies were written in his lifetime, and any enquiry of the kind I have made would have been very painful to him. Even now, I am conscious of some apparent violation of human decencies in this stage of my enquiry, although the critical events took place more than a century ago. In any case, I have pursued my line of investigation because in this way alone could I find any satisfactory explanation of what made him the man he was. I am inclined to be suspicious of much psycho-biography, believing that it often involves the imposition of *a priori* textbook reasoning on specific subjects without sufficiently allowing their lives to speak for themselves, and often drawing conclusions on the basis of very inadequate evidence. In writing an earlier work on Arthur Conan Doyle I discussed his background, but had insufficient data to attempt anything like psycho-biography, even had I been inclined to: it was a matter of showing how his youthful surroundings played a part in the making of his literary work at a later stage. But in de Valera's case I have no alternative: the special circumstances of his origin demand such a method. I have not invited specialists in psychoanalysis to prompt my reasoning, but have simply used my reading, my observation and my inheritance as what he would have called one of the plain people of Ireland. In this study it would have been sheer folly, as well as very tiresome, to attempt to distance myself from my Irish Catholic peasant roots. I am one of his own, looking at him, I hope without becoming too parochial for my other readers.

Having followed his career to the Easter Rising, with some special emphasis on the man who brought him there—again, a factor oddly underemphasized in earlier writing—I have given close study to his life from then to the Anglo-Irish Treaty of 1921. Although he was central to the events of these years, he actually lived outside Ireland for much of them, either in gaol or in the United States. I have tried to account for his behaviour then, paying particular attention to the role of the extraordinary magnetism of America for him. It seems to me that the patterns formed in his life up to the Treaty determined his subsequent development fairly clearly. At all events, I have dealt much more cursorily with his subsequent history, and have treated it thematically after his elevation to power in the Irish Free State in 1932. I have paid particular attention to his Catholicism and its relationship to issues of Church and State: while Ireland had a large share of Catholic politicians, his case seems unique among them for certain reasons of origin. I have looked more briefly at other major questions of his public life. Although my study of his rise to fame imparted some new ways of looking at his later accomplishments, the existence of several valuable new studies on aspects of his later life enabled me to summarize rather than explore at this point. To say something really new for that period will necessitate the study of his private papers which are currently closed. These may, of course, yield important new material on his early life, but I doubt if what I have recorded here of its basic contours will be greatly changed.

I have opened and closed with poems which establish certain moods for me. The poem by James Stephens was written and published during the Treaty debates of December—January 1921-22: I find it fascinating as being so strongly in contrast in its values from those given to its recipient by his background, and it furnishes in the context a rather melancholy music for his story. The poem by Rudyard Kipling at the conclusion is not proposed as a parallel to de Valera's life, but the similarity of certain of the symbols strikes me forcibly: it says things about him that I cannot reach. Kipling was antithetical to almost all that de Valera stood for, politically, and he had little prose sympathy with the subject of the poem, Napoleon:

in verse he caught certain qualities of human understanding which partly account for his outstanding popularity in de Valera's Ireland. James Stephens (not to be confused with the homonymous founder of Fenianism in the nineteenth century) was a friend of Thomas MacDonagh and introduced his collected poems. I think that he did not know de Valera well; he may have made his acquaintance through Arthur Griffith, a friend of his, or perhaps through MacDonagh. His *The Insurrection in Dublin* is one of the best eye-witness accounts of the Easter Rising.

OWEN DUDLEY EDWARDS
Edinburgh, January 1987

Acknowledgements

My mother, Síle Ní Shúilleabháin, died a few days after sending me Father
Seán Farragher's *Dev and his Alma Mater* which proved to be my most
valuable source; her encouragement has been my great strength at all times
and I have tried to follow her guidance in keeping this a very Munster view
of its subject. I went for advice as she would have told me, to Professors
Joseph Lee and John A. Murphy of University College Cork: each has
given the typescript a most careful reading, extracted me from pitfalls, and
made vital corrections. She would have been as entertained by their
comments as I was; I thank them on her behalf as well as on mine.

Mr Allan Boyd has given me wise advice and inspiration, read both
typescript and proofs critically and carefully, and without the inspiration
of his ideals on books this would have been much weaker.

Dr Kenneth Owen Morgan has been an editor far greater than I deserve.
It has been a rare privilege to have had his guidance, patience, kindness,
wisdom and most valuable criticism.

Professor Brian Farrell's writing inspired my initial perception of the
subject, and his advice at an early stage was of the greatest help to me.

My father, Professor Robert Dudley Edwards, commented on many
questions with characteristic zest and unrivalled knowledge. He first
taught me to consider de Valera historically in his articles on that question
in the *Leader* in 1956, as he taught me so much of historical method. But
this book also testifies to his work in another capacity: as a collector of oral
evidence. I have found my recollection of innumerable pieces of
information recorded by him to be invaluable. I have ventured to make this
my tribute to his great services as an Irish historian, in which I join so many
of his students and colleagues.

Mr Dónall Ó Luanaigh, Keeper of Printed Books of the National

Library of Ireland, obtained and copied for me Hanna Sheehy-Skeffington's obituary of Catherine (de Valera) Wheelwright. His kindness is in the true tradition of his institution which has taught me so much.

I am embarrassed to think of all I owe to the National Library of Scotland, whose patience, good nature, and resourcefulness are as always endless.

I am deeply grateful also to the staffs of the Library of the University of Edinburgh, and of the British Library.

I thank my colleagues of the North American Studies Seminar of my University, especially Professor G. A. Shepperson, Dr Rhodri Jeffreys-Jones, Dr Adam Naylor, and Dr Colin Affleck. I thank my hosts at the Irish Association in Belfast, Dr Christopher and Ms Joyce McGimpsey, and my chairman, Mr Brian Garrett, and the members. All proved most encouraging when I gave papers on part of this subject to each institution.

I cannot possibly indicate all I owe to my wife, Bonnie Dudley Edwards, my mother-in-law, Elizabeth Balbirnie Lee, my children Leila, Sara and Michael, and our friend Mark Kennedy, all of whom coped splendidly with de Valera's omnipresence in our home.

Nobody except myself is responsible for any shortcomings that will be discovered in these pages. Still less responsible (if possible) are the many people who were not consulted but whose advice and knowledge have been of the greatest benefit to me over many years. I fear deeply that this book may hurt one of the best adult friends of my childhood, Dr Maurice Moynihan; I hope he will still let me record my love and gratitude to him. Professor Thomas P. O'Neill is another very generous old friend who will not agree with what is here, but to whom my personal and historiographical obligations are outstanding. These are de Valera's gallant defenders; among his noblest critics my love and appreciation of Dr León Ó Broin stand now as always.

I thank many other intellectual creditors, invaluable if unwitting: among the dead, my grandmother, Brigid Teresa Dudley Edwards; my uncle, James Wall; my godmother, Mary Carty; Owen Sheehy-Skeffington; Desmond Ryan; Seán MacEntee; Máighréad MacEntee; An t-Uachtarán Cearbhall Ó Dalaigh; Joseph Count Plunkett; Tarlach Ó Raifeartaigh; Seán Gibbons; Niall Gibbons; Monsignor Pádraig de Brún; James Carty; Frank Gallagher; Alexis FitzGerald; Peadar O'Donnell; James O'Beirne; Noël Hartnett; John Belton; F.S.L. Lyons. I thank in their own selves, my aunt, Elizabeth Wall; my sister Mary Dudley Edwards; my sister Ruth Dudley Edwards; Máire Cruise O'Brien; Conor Cruise O'Brien; Aindreas

Ó Gallchoir; Mae Moynihan; Terence de Vere White; Douglas Gageby; Noël Browne; Alf Mac Lochlainn; Fionnuala Mac Lochlainn; R.F. Foster; Bill Meek; Michael Williams; Ronan Fanning; Donal McCartney; Revd F.X. Martin, O.S.A.; Revd Anthony Ross, O.P.; Aedan O'Beirne; John Bowman; David Harkness; Winifred Ewing; Brian Lenihan; Revd Noel O'Donoghue, O.Carm.; John Pocock; Tom Dunne; T.J. Barron; J.H. Whyte; Patrick Lynch; Martin Cowley; Basil Megaw; Terence Brown; Mary Bromage; Charles Neu; Breandán Mac Giolla Choille; Patrick Henchy; Thomas N. Brown; David Doyle; John Arnott; Fergus Pyle; Maurice Leitch; Michael Viney; Garret Fitzgerald; James Downey.

The early part of this work was written at Hawkesyard Priory, Rugely, Staffordshire, and I thank my friends of the Spode House Family Week who discussed and greatly inspired the earliest version, as well as the Dominicans who built up the excellent library where I worked so happily.

Prologue by James Stephens

Minuette:
On the Freedom of Ireland—To Éamonn de Valera
(Poblacht na h-Éireann, 3 January 1922)

I

The moon shines,
And the wind blows,
And the heart knows,

Carelessly, and carelessly!
That to them each thing inclines,
And that everything is free!

All that is, is given to thee!
Take the love, that comes and goes!
Uncomplaining, thankless, be,

As the moon, the bird, the rose,
Thankless, uncomplaining, are
Beauty, Music, and a Star!

II

Call, and come, and come, and call!
Nothing is denied the gay!
All to each, and each to all.

Fall, and flow, and go away;
As the moon shines, and the heart knows;
Carelessly, as the wind blows!

Not for duty we fulfil
Lovely motions—'tis for naught!
All the will of good and ill,

All of ignorance, and thought,
All are harmless, if we are
Free as Wind, and Rose, and Star.

III

Taking all of cherishing
That befall, or may not fall,
As a happy, chancing, thing,

Some for each, and all for all;
Taking all the haps that be,
Carelessly, and carelessly!

Life comes on, with not a word;
Love is love, on no demand;
Death, unasked, hath him bestirred,

Lifting all up by the hand:
All that fall he stoops above
Lovingly, for he is love!

IV

Love is round, and round, and round!
Everywhere, in every spot,
It is lost, and it is found,

Here it is—and here is not!
Man, and beast, and bird, and snake,
Take, and take, and take, and take,

As the Moon takes up the sight!
As the Rose takes up the shower!
As the Heart takes all Delight,

Might and Beauty for its dower!
All that is—for all is free—
Take carelessly, and carelessly!

1

The Reign of Melchisedech

But Melchisedech the king of Salem, bringing forth bread and wine, for he was the priest of the most high God,

Blessed him, and said: Blessed be Abram by the most high God, who created heaven and earth.

And blessed be the most high God, by whose protection thy enemies are in thy hands. And he gave him the tithes of all.

—Genesis, 14: 18—20 (Douay)

For this Melchisedech was king of Salem, priest of the most high God, who met Abraham returning from the slaughter of the kings and blessed him;

To whom also Abraham divided the tithes of all; who first indeed by interpretation is king of justice; and then also king of Salem, that is, king of peace;

Without father, without mother, without genealogy, having neither beginning of days nor end of life, but likened unto the Son of God, continueth a priest for ever.

Now consider how great this man is, to whom also Abraham the patriarch gave tithes out of the principal things.

—Hebrews, 7: 1—4 (Douay)

The history of Éamon de Valera is in great part the history of Ireland from 1916 to 1959. Born in 1882, he was elected President of Sinn Féin in October 1917. The following year it captured a majority of Irish seats in the elections for the House of Commons of the United Kingdom of Great Britain and Ireland. He was unanimously chosen as President of Dáil Éireann, by its members, sitting as an assembly which consisted of the Members of Parliament who refused to occupy their seats in Westminster; he served from 1 April 1919 to 7 January 1922. He was quite inaccurately identified with the leadership of violent Republican opposition to the Anglo-Irish Treaty, although he certainly had opposed it, had resigned his Presidency of Dáil Éireann on account of it and was in rank a very minor subaltern in the guerrilla forces warring against the Irish Free State established under it. He remained President of Sinn Féin until he resigned on 11 March 1926 because it had opposed on principle his tactical decision to enter the Free State Dáil. He was supported widely, and became President of an organization, Fianna Fáil, which as a political party formed a government in 1932. He was thus President of the Executive Council of the Irish Free State, but his title was altered to Taoiseach (chieftain) of Eire under the new Constitution he produced and saw ratified in 1937: he remained in power until 1948. He became President of the Council of the League of Nations in 1932, and President of the Assembly of the League of Nations in 1938. He served as Leader of the Opposition in Dáil Éireann from 1948 to 1951, during which period the name of the state was altered to the Republic of Ireland (Dáil Éireann as an assembly without Westminster and international recognition from 1919 to 1922 had declared itself to be the representative assembly of 'the Irish Republic'). He returned to power in 1951, fell in 1954, and regained power in 1957, serving until

1959, when he relinquished office as Taoiseach and was elected to what, in contrast to his earlier Presidencies (including those in the League of Nations), was the largely ceremonial post of President of the Republic of Ireland. He was re-elected in 1966 and finally left office in 1973. He died in 1975.

The recitation of all of these Presidencies has a slightly ironic ring, taken in conjunction with his birth in the United States, a country whose little boys were taught to dream that they might some day be President. The title also seems to haunt subsequent historians of de Valera. The fact that his last Presidency was a ceremonial one has invited the thought that he presided over his Ireland, rather than directing it (although nobody seems to deny that he made much more of his Presidencies in the League of Nations than was customary for other holders of those offices). The United States Presidency, the Presidency he did not get, combines the ceremonial role of modern monarch with the executive leadership of a Prime Minister, and students of its incumbents will argue whether each one primarily reigned or ruled. For all of de Valera's hold on the attention and imagination of his fellow-Irish, at home and abroad, and of the many persons in near or remote corners of the world who were interested in Ireland, the question is there, as are its corollaries—if he did not rule, who or what did, and how much, and for how long?

But whether he ruled or not, he held the imagination of his fellow-Irish and of many others, evoking admiration and emulation, or detestation and execration. He may not have shaped his Ireland to the extent that contemporaries believed: he certainly shaped it in the minds of those contemporaries. As a person, his actual impact was limited; as a force, an epiphany, it was extraordinary. He was a symbol to his times of revolution and stability. The historian may periodize the phases dominated by each; contemporaries never fully separated the symbols. His first steps towards revolutionary leadership seemed governed by mathematical logic; his last political meeting wallowed in obeisance to the memory of the 1916 insurrection and thrilled to the song celebrating the taking up of arms against a popularly elected Irish government in 1922, 'The Legion of the Rearguard'. He demanded a united, indivisible island absolutely independent of Britain, and in practice settled so clearly for control of 26 out of 32 counties that Northern Ireland seems to have had little meaning for him save as a diplomatic weapon to achieve his ends within those 26. He demanded a full restoration of Irish Gaelic as the first language of Ireland, but again settled in practice for the language being used as a means of ensuring an old pre-independence civil service could not continue in power through its own heirs and disciples without perpetual deference to new cultural norms.

His most astonishing achievement in the eyes of the world must have been his part in the acquisition, preservation and extension of Irish independence, despite the dangerous proximity, deep cultural ties, vital economic links and similarity of many international interests, to the larger island. Because he survived so many who had played comparable and at times greater parts in these matters, he came to symbolize much of what had been the work of others. In particular, much of Michael Collins's achievement had been more significant in the winning of so much independence in 1921 and the establishment of a momentum which would ensure the gaining of more: but because Collins supported the Anglo-Irish Treaty and de Valera opposed it, the more revolutionary figure was cast for a more conservative reputation by his friends and enemies alike. Collins was killed soon after the Civil War began in the summer of 1922. Collins's supporters on the treaty issue included writers of history who were more radical on several issues than de Valera was—Desmond Ryan on socialism, P.S. O'Hegarty on religion, León Ó Broin on the restoration of the Irish language—but despite their work de Valera held the radical high ground in most minds.

Similarly, the de Valera government of the 1930s was much more the heir of the Cosgrave government of 1922–32 than W.T. Cosgrave, de Valera or their respective supporters would admit: the concept of state intervention went back to Cosgrave's day, so did the independence and forceful stance in foreign affairs, so did the ruthlessness towards civil liberties, the enactment of literary censorship and the outlawry of divorce, while de Valera's exercises in economic protectionism in the 1930s realized the economic thought of Arthur Griffith, who opposed him on the Treaty and supplanted him as President of Dáil Éireann. Professor Brian Farrell has argued that in cabinet the quiet and uncharismatic Cosgrave was actually a much more forceful leader than de Valera: the 1920s' cabinets were swayed by the President, the 1930s saw much more consideration of the views of Ministers. But Ireland and the world assumed de Valera's cabinet to be composed simply of de Valera's men all under his direction, whereas Cosgrave's team, with such exotic figures as Ernest Blythe, Richard Mulcahy, Joseph McGrath, Kevin O'Higgins, Patrick Hogan, Desmond FitzGerald, Patrick McGilligan, John Marcus O'Sullivan, Eoin O'Duffy, seemed far less easily ruled.

The paradox may supply the answer. Not only did Cosgrave face this formidable array of subordinates, but he was very conscious of his lack of

lustre compared to his predecessors Collins and Griffith who had both died
in August 1922, to say nothing of de Valera himself, still formidably living.
Hence he had to impose his will, if he was not to go under. Fianna Fáil's
whole existence stemmed from de Valera's personal following, hence he
had no need to insist on it. As President of Dáil Éireann from 1919 to 1922
he had been for much of the time in jail or in the United States: but when he
was at work his style of Presidency had also been one of presiding. The
1930s and 1940s continued the pattern. He took care to know his men and
their views rather better; he had been so little in touch with the Ministers in
the Dáil Éireann cabinet that the discovery he would be outvoted there on
the issue of the Anglo-Irish Treaty apparently was a surprise to him. But
the world in 1919–21 saw the President more than any other figure, all the
more because of his sensational jailbreak and his American campaign, and
the world in the 1930s and 1940s confused the fealty of his Ministers with
subservience. The early 1940s, with war censorship in Ireland and abroad,
saw him misunderstood even more: de Valera was actually much more
sympathetic to the Americans, and even to the British, than were some of
his Ministers and many of his followers; but his reputation led observers to
assume he had far more freedom to manoeuvre than was really the case.
Irish failure to support the Allies was, therefore, blamed on de Valera,
whose position (and, indeed, vanity) prevented his showing how fortunate
the Allies were in having him where he was, and how weak his hand at times
seemed to him to be at home as well as abroad. The appearance of firm rule
was an indispensable weapon to him: its effectiveness was enhanced by the
freedom he was careful to accord to his followers provided they catered to
the image. Cartoonists portrayed him as an engine-driver, and the
simplicity of the interpretation was generally appealing: 'Daddy's in the
Engine', ran *Dublin Opinion's* caption, and nobody sought to work out
how old Daddy's family was getting and how much of the driving it was
really doing. Even in the 1950s his insistence on clinging to leadership was
assumed to mean a maintenance of autocratic rule: it was because there was
so little autocracy that he was enabled to last so long. In electoral terms, it
suited both him and his party that he should be the main issue, and the main
vote-getter, most of the time. The rallying cry 'Up Dev!' was the motion
for debate in Irish politics for forty years. It seemed to make no allowance
for change in time or attitude; in fact it made great allowances.

So, even if de Valera's leadership was in matters of detail more apparent
than real, the symbolism of that leadership was of the greatest importance
in itself. His personal situation, in particular, symbolized the break with
Britain: his birth was American, his name was Spanish, his preferred

language was Irish, and even his vocation of the study of mathematics lay outside the normal interests of the British ruling class. De Valera's Ireland took some pleasure in the thought that its leader took his relaxation with Rowan Hamilton's theory of quaternions as opposed to huntin', shootin' and fishin'. He seemed anything but English. Again, appearance was not altogether true to reality. De Valera was the heir to much that was English, and maintained much of that; his enjoyment of bad jokes about Scotsmen was very English. He had, after all, grown up in a highly Anglified country, however much he formally denied any force in that fact, save in the negative sense that it taught him what symbols to oppose. But he was much more cautious about tampering with substance. Even as a revolutionary his dependence on militaristic symbolism was a desperate attempt to rival in its own terms the culture whence he sought to lead an escape.

The recital of these matters still deepens the problem. If de Valera's leadership was in so many ways symbol rather than substance, why should it have received so passionate a response? The answer here lies in the realm of shadow and spirit. De Valera came to be perceived as a form of priest-king, like David, Solomon or particularly Melchisedech. Only de Gaulle offers a similar case in the twentieth century (Makarios is an instructive comparison, but his leadership status followed instead of preceded his priesthood); Washington and Napoleon show such features in the remoter past, though in both cases their status is linked as de Valera's was not, to military achievements. The most de Valera had to offer there was his holding operation in Boland's Mills in the Dublin insurrection of 1916, but that whole episode of the Easter Week Rising acquired its force for spiritual rather than military reasons. De Valera had certain qualities in common with Gandhi, with Lenin, and with Mao. But he was not a prophet, or a saint, or an original theoretician: he was, at his best, a master of the dry, ironic perception of unpleasant, but avoidable, alternatives. He was ascetic and it amused him to be thought more ascetic than he was. He enjoyed refining an original doctrine and would, when he chose, do so to a point of tortuous pedantry. The saints and theoreticians, loosely lumped together in a totality, were largely comprehended by the martyrs of the Easter Rising: others were added during the Anglo-Irish war of 1919–21 and the Irish Civil War of 1922–23. De Valera knew the importance of selectivity in extolling their theories. Patrick Pearse received virtually divine honours among the martyrs, and his cult became the mortar in the political theology erected by de Valera and his followers.[1] As priest-king, de Valera set the seal on veneration of the martyrs.

The Irish Catholics over whom he reigned were accustomed to largely unvarying ritual in their formal, weekly (sometimes daily) and very devout expressions of religious belief: his own politico-religious ceremonial also emphasized ritual, and his preaching was orthodox and fundamentalist. Outside the ritual, he shared with Melchisedech an alien and uncertain origin, an enigmatic situation: but his sacerdotal function, again like Melchisedech's, was clear and independent, unimprisoned by any identification with lines of ideological descent from either the Irish Republican Brotherhood (the Irish official Fenian organization) or Arthur Griffith's Sinn Féin. The analogy with Melchisedech may puzzle readers of Protestant origin, accustomed as they may be to obscure Biblical texts: but Melchisedech appears in the Canon of the Mass, as the original celebrant to bring forth bread and wine for sacrifice. The Sacrifice of Christ, Who died for mankind, is perpetuated in the Mass by the priest consecrating bread and wine; the sacrifice of the martyrs who died for Ireland was perpetuated in public ceremonial and invocation by de Valera. The assumption in both cases was that perpetual faith in the efficacy of the priest was required lest the original sacrifice be dishonoured by blasphemy. Catholics were taught that by apostasy Christ was recrucified; the same implicit assumption lay behind the horror at any sign of apostasy to the tenets of de Valera. The annual contemplation of Christ's passion and suffering renewed Catholic faith; similar contemplation of the Easter martyrs' wounds (Connolly's leg, wounded in the fighting, gangrened at the time of his execution, and Cathal Brugha's wounds in the South Dublin Union fighting which were believed to have been so bad that his execution was deemed unnecessary), suffering (the hunger-strike until death of Cork Lord Mayor Terence MacSwiney in 1920), and deaths, renewed political faith. De Valera himself officiated in his priestly function with austerity and dignity over such matters: he could rest assured that the martyrology in its gory detail was well disseminated before his people by such publicists as Brian O'Higgins and Frank Gallagher. But he carried his function through with appropriate word and gesture.

Relatives of the martyrs were cherished and elevated in the political movement according to their talents: Pearse's sister and Connolly's daughter were made Senators, Tom Clarke's widow became Lord Mayor of Dublin, Erskine Childers's son was put in the Cabinet. In 1966 de Valera as Chancellor of the National University of Ireland had honorary degrees conferred on the next of kin to the signatories of the 1916 Proclamation. (One declined, on rigidly Republican principles.) In all of this, the 'plain people of Ireland', as de Valera liked to call them, did not explicitly cite the analogy with the priest-king Melchisedech and probably did not think of it.

But their religious training conditioned them to respond to de Valera as a Melchisedech figure. The whole, highly mystical, business was not a matter for thought and analysis. If anything, Irish Catholics would be more ready to speculate about their Catholic doctrines than about de Valera's political parallel to Catholic practice. De Valera's political opponents in Ireland might privately detest the cults, but their chief response was to imitate them: Cosgrave's followers produced cults of Griffith, Collins and Kevin O'Higgins, Labour sought somewhat gingerly to reclaim Connolly while being much more uneasy with his Socialism than was de Valera, secure in the selectivity of his texts.

De Valera's relationship with the Roman Catholic church was thus from the outset a very curious one: he needed it not only for its stability, its non-Englishness, its relationship to Irish nationalist identity, but also as the parent oak on which his parasite political religion grew. Yet both he and certain ecclesiastical authorities resented one another: the priest-king knew that some priests made inroads on his authority at least to the extent of requiring personal loyalties which might not always recognize his spiritual predominance, the priests in their hearts knew the dangers to them of a politician largely using their theological coinage for his secular purposes. Even when de Valera obtained an Archbishop of Dublin, John Charles McQuaid, of his own personal preference, the teacher of his sons and the headmaster of the school where he had studied and taught, the alliance did not last for even a decade. There was very little practical divergence between de Valera's views and the attitudes of the united Catholic hierarchy in his time, once he had re-entered constitutional politics in 1927. Although Cosgrave's party had the name of being clericalist much more than did Fianna Fáil, de Valera's Constitution of 1937 was singled out as the leading expression of political Catholicism in contemporary Europe, in contrast to the secularism of that under which Cosgrave governed.[2] The problem for the bishops was that de Valera was much too good a Catholic, and one who, as a politician, saw that Catholicism was too valuable to be left to the bishops.

The Catholicism of de Valera's party and movement had two major origins, one popular, the other personal. Religion in Ireland in de Valera's lifetime was an intensely popular matter, Sabbath observance among Catholics, Protestants and Jews being probably the highest in the world. The eighteenth century had involved cruel and demeaning civil disabilities for Irish Catholics and only slightly less harsh ones for the Presbyterians. The latter religion was a popularly-based one; the former became so. Religion dictated caste. The late Maureen Wall established that the penal legislation pressed less harshly in practice than in theory,[3] but the stigma of being the lowest form of humanity, if that, was remembered down the generations. The Catholics, driven out of landholding, went into commerce in many cases, and with Catholic emancipation in the late eighteenth and early nineteenth centuries came a slow bourgeoisification of Irish Catholicism and administrative inculcation of clerical efficiency. Catholic clerical aims and Catholic nationalist ones did not always coincide, but they were largely made to do so in the social and constitutional agitations of Parnell in the 1880s as they had been in the 1820s when the struggle for the final stage of Catholic emancipation was led by Daniel O'Connell. O'Connell can claim to have made the Catholic populace the first mass political movement in the world; under Parnell, the grandchild of that movement was streamlined into a national machine. It atrophied and fell, but the pattern of its activity was there for the Sinn Féin party which displaced it in 1918. The clergy were still being asked to adjust themselves to a revolutionary situation, firstly with the fall of their allies in the Irish Parliamentary Party and the rise of Sinn Féin, self-appointed heirs to what had been in its time a very unpopular insurrection in 1916. Dáil Éireann certainly chose to proceed through obvious forms of non-violent resistance; but it was unable to control votaries of violence which it belatedly sanctioned. The Catholic priests had to consider the dictates of moral responsibility and the dangers of alienating their flocks, who reacted angrily against British governmental repression. By 1921 the bishops had come to terms with Dáil Éireann's leadership, but they heartily welcomed the Anglo-Irish Treaty and hence turned their wrath on de Valera and his followers who opposed it in arms in 1922. The very fact that many clerics had turned something of a blind eye to excesses of the Irish Volunteers, nominally controlled by Dáil Éireann, meant that now they had a popularly-based Irish government to support, they would be all the more intransigent in dealing with its opponents. The Irish Republican Army, as the anti-Treaty forces called themselves, were excommunicated.

Such action had been taken against violent patriotic movements in the past, notably the Fenians, and the effect was to confirm the natural tendency of many of them to reject all supernatural religion. That would also be the case for many opponents of the Treaty, but de Valera's followers who ultimately accepted entry into the Free State Dáil in 1927 were by their nature persons who believed in a recovery of stability, however much on their terms. Their social origins were, sometimes, lower than those of the Fenians had been—de Valera himself came from the lowest class, the labourers—and they confronted a church welded into

Irish society by highly modernized organisation. Above all, most of them simply did not want to be outside the Church. The ease with which they happily consecrated their lives to two Churches, de Valera's and the Bishops', is a proof of that desire. Fianna Fáil began its career by meeting outside church gates after Mass, with the support of the local clergy where they could get it. De Valera and his ministers knew that the Bishops would prefer the more conservative government of Cosgrave, witness de Valera's satisfaction at the promotion of a cleric of his choice in McQuaid's case. But while with their past record of excommunication de Valera's followers knew that their attendance at Mass was essential, the main emphasis should be on the personal commitment of most of them. Their religion was a popular one, sanctified by years of persecution: Catholics were socially below the salt until very late in the nineteenth century because they were Catholics, and popular tradition execrated those who had 'turned' to gain the benefits of apostacy in the eighteenth century, even those who had 'turned' to get food in the great famine of 1845–49. They were where they were politically, as they saw it, because they were who they were religiously. The vehemence of their sense of Irishness was essentially part of their Catholicism.

Let us take one example of what men meant by their devotion to de Valera. Robert Briscoe was not Catholic but Jewish, and was a life-long adherent of de Valera. Association strengthened their affection. In the 1930s, the Cosgrave supporters included some extreme clerical-Fascist elements of anti-Semitic attitude, and de Valera was attacked by his most scurrilous clericalist enemies for having a Jew as a political intimate. In fact, Briscoe was not appointed a Minister, although he did become Dublin's Lord Mayor, in which post he was a roaring success. When he was dying, he lay in a coma for days without moving a muscle. Eventually de Valera, old and blind, was led to the bedside. The crackling clear tones spoke to the man in the bed, the man whom all who could see took to be wholly beyond reach: 'Bob?' The blind man's hand took the hand of the patient. 'Do you know me, Bob?' And from the figure pronounced unconscious for all of the previous week came, desperately weak but wholly audible: 'The Chief!' Briscoe died the next day or so.

For such a devotee and his countless if more lowly counterparts there can be given, as de Valera in his mathematical mood would put it, the converse. One witticism ran: 'Why is it that no street in Dublin has been dedicated to the memory of de Valera, although we have Griffith Avenue, and Collins Avenue?' 'Because no street exists which is long enough, narrow enough, or crooked enough.' De Valera was tall, and was popularly known as 'the

Long Fellow', perhaps in contrast to Michael Collins, 'the Big Fellow'.
'Crooked' is an obvious form of reproach, visited upon every controversial
democratic leader of the day from Lloyd George to Franklin Roosevelt.
But 'narrow' was rather neat. De Valera's political theology knew little
ecumenism: neither did the Catholicism of his political lifetime.

James Dillon was the son of the last leader of the Irish Parliamentary
Party, and he himself sat in the Costello cabinets. He was a parliamen-
tarian of unsurpassed grandiloquence, not merely archaic but elegant,
witty and unfailingly sure-footed. Douglas Gageby, the editor of the *Irish
Times,* a paper by now liberal but which for thirty years after the Treaty
had been an indignant mourner for the death of the Union of Great Britain
and Ireland, had never met de Valera and one day told Dillon he was
shortly so to do. 'You will be a changed man henceforward', intoned
Dillon. Gageby said that men might come and men might go, but he would
preserve his independence, or words to that effect. Dillon shook his head.
'You cannot remain the same. You will have been in the presence of the
enchanter.' Was he thinking of Pitt's description of being with Fox as
being under the wand of the magician? Almost certainly. He would have
had too much *amour-propre* not to supply synonyms in place of the
original, too much sense of the occasion not to summon up his formidable
learning of the literary classics (in this case Macaulay's life of the younger
Pitt). And he would have enjoyed seeing himself and de Valera as Pitt and
Fox, he being a man for the western alliance and conservatism, de Valera as
he saw it being a dangerous neutral, and a fomenter of pestiferous
ideologies. And there was the familial tradition of political emnity: de
Valera had in person no less than in party defeated John Dillon in 1918. But
it was de Valera, Dillon's Fox, who held supreme power in Irish assemblies
for 24 years, a period longer than Pitt, while Dillon, like so many men of
talent in de Valera's political lifetime, wasted his gifts out of office for
most of his life, as Fox had done.

I only saw de Valera once, although he dominated the Ireland in which I
grew up. It was his last political speech, as it took place in 1959 at the end of
his first campaign for the Presidency. (His second campaign for the
Presidency, that of 1966, was orchestrated by Fianna Fáil as an act of
homage required of the people. It was a dangerous device, as it proved, and
Dublin would vote against him, leaving him with a much narrower victory.
It was in reality a warning to his party, still in power, not to get above itself:
the Presidential election has been used for that purpose since that time, and
probably will be again. But de Valera was hurt, and showed it in his
interview on television after the announcement of his victory. He said he

had always regarded himself as a country person, and therefore he was happy the country had voted for him. He was right in perceiving that Dublin had moved far away. In fact, his highly urban successor, Seán Lemass, was to prove a more dangerous figure to his reputation in the eyes of subsequent historians than Cosgrave (whose substantial services and remarkable character still await a biographer) or Costello (whose team certainly cleared up much that had gone to seed in de Valera's long reign). Lemass, who actually died before him although many years his junior, now overshadows his former Chief, especially in the eyes of economic historians: the hard-bitten pragmatist seems a breath of fresh air after the mystical archaism of his predecessor.)

De Valera's long-overdue retirement to the Presidency was being eagerly awaited by his contemporaries when he faced that last political meeting in 1959, but he showed no sign of it. He must indeed have been almost totally blind at this point, and his eyesight had been very bad for the previous two decades, but it was never mentioned publicly or in print, even by the most envenomed of his opponents. The location of de Valera's 1959 meeting was in College Green, which offered the mixture of open and secret symbolism characteristic of de Valera's reliance on the unspoken even more than the spoken word, when the unspoken was to his advantage. Officially the location was a tribute to the former presence of the Irish Parliament in the building behind the meeting up to its extinction in the Act of Union with Great Britain in 1800. Actually it also symbolized defiance of the old order, as represented by Trinity College Dublin, across the street. Trinity was the Protestant University founded by Elizabeth I, and bastion of Irish Unionism. De Valera had carefully and shrewdly nurtured it as an object lesson of former alien rule. The meeting actually symbolized defiance of the old Raj in a sense different from that intended by de Valera: Lemass had no interest in investing money for the education of archaic Irish Unionists and their English clients, and when he came to power Trinity was given a stiff quota of Irish places to be met. Self-assured and unpretentious Dublin accents now fill the quadrangles which in 1959 still echoed to loud English upper-class voices.

De Valera had placed before the electorate two issues, the Presidential election, and a referendum to abolish proportional representation, his guarantee to his party that despite his translation to the Presidency they would remain in power. Proportional representation threatened their hegemony, they thought (a fairly ungenerous response to a system which had given them 21 years in power under de Valera, and a revelation of the insecurity they felt when deprived of his leadership at election-time). The

campaign had been extremely bitter, its opening salvos including various
legal and constitutional disputes, and all other parties had sunk their
differences to defend PR. The final Fianna Fáil meeting was a failure:
Dublin would vote massively in favour of PR on the morrow, although on
this occasion it would also vote for de Valera to be president. But the
meeting acknowledged little change in Dublin from the old politics of
mystique and martyrdom: Dublin, on its side, was more interested in slum
clearance than referendums, and was at least able to say as much by voting
'No'. De Valera's surviving followers from the Civil War days paraded and
the proceedings began with 'the Legion of the Rearguard'.

> Lurid the morning, with flame and shot and shell,
> Now rally, Ireland, your sons that love you well!
> Pledged they'll defend you, though death or prison cell
> Wait for the Legion of the Rearguard.
>
> Up the Republic! Hear their battle-cry!
> Pearse, Clarke, MacDermott still pray for you on high
> Ready and willing for love of you to die,
> Now march ye, Legion of the Rearguard!
>
> Legion of the Re-ar-guard, ans'ring Ireland's call,
> See them close around you, from Cork to Donegal.
> Tone and Emmet guide you, though the way be hard.
> De Valera leads you, Soldiers of the Legion of the Rearguard!

The first speaker was Kevin Boland, nephew of Harry Boland, one of the
first prominent martyrs in the Civil War among de Valera's followers: he
delivered a speech against Proportional Representation, of monumental
tedium. (He would resign from the Fianna Fáil party eleven years later in
protest against the dismissal of two colleagues for alleged gun-running to
Northern Ireland.) He was followed by Patrick Pearse's sister, Margaret, a
Senator, whose speech was certainly not tedious: 'This system of
Proportional Representation was foisted on ye by the British. Throw it
back in their faces!' She pointed out that if the dead who died for Ireland
were there today, it was upon this platform they would be. And she
introduced the Chief.

De Valera made no allusion to the rites which preceded his remarks: they
were expected to have done their work, as had always been the case, and he
now did his. It was, again as was customary, the didactic schoolmaster at
work. The voice was dry, and now crackled with age, but clear and strong.
He retained the accent of south Limerick where he had grown up, its
aspirate 'r' and whistling 'l', sounds found in the Welsh language but not in

Irish or English. He had the intrusive 'i', almost a subscript, which is employed by speakers of good Irish between labial and liquid consonants and is among many little devices that go to make it one of the most beautiful languages in the world. 'When you go tomorrow to the polling booth'—surely a Welsh speaker would have been charmed by the hiss behind that double 'l'—'you will approach the Returning Officer. He will request your polling card. It is desirable to have this card with you, but it is not necessary, and should you chance to have lost or mislaid it, you will so inform him. He will hand you two papers, a white paper and a brown paper. You will take these papers to the polling booth, where you will obtain a pencil. Taking the pencil in your right hand, unless you should happen to be left-handed, you will mark the letter or symbol 'X' upon the brown paper opposite the word 'YES', and upon the white paper you will put the figure or digit '1' . . .' 'Oppósite yew' roared a voice from the crowd, whether in ecstasy or irony it was unclear. 'Opposite the candidate of your choice' replied de Valera dulcetly, to loud cheers and laughter. Whether his hecklers interrupted in fealty or hostility, he was never the man to lose the chance to cap them and capture the crowd applause.

Then Seán MacEntee spoke. Evidently bored by the earlier proceedings, he capitalized on his personal unpopularity to arouse hostile heckling, vigorously replied to it, incited further disturbance, encouraged the police to remove it (which it did as best it could) and the meeting broke up in some degree of disorder, after the singing of the National Anthem which coincidentally bears the first line '*Sinn-ne Fianna Fáil*' and is very loosely translated

> Soldiers are we
> Whose lives are pledged to Ireland.
> Some have come
> From a land beyond the wave . . .

It was over. It was, in reality, all over. Later Fianna Fáil leaders would try to bring back that harmony of stability and revolution: the lion of Republicanism in 1959 was permitted a roar and a stretch while being held in the firmest of reins, but the lion, reawakened later, would prove beyond control and prone to control its new masters. But in one sense de Valera had no successor. The priest-kingship died when he retired. And he was retiring. Win or lose—he is unlikely to have doubted he would win—this would be his last political meeting. He seemed certain that the Presidency for him would be non-political, as it had been for his predecessors since 1937. Seán Lemass, it turned out, was even more certain of it.

But he had travelled a long, long road since the day, nearly three-quarters of a century earlier, when he had come from that land beyond the wave.

2

The Man from God Knows Where

I am not of your faith. I am, as you well know, of a particular faith of which I am probably the only member of this great hall. But I would like to say to you good Christians that if it was right for you to accept as your Savior a man born in a stable, surely we Irish have the same right to accept as our leader a great man, no matter how lowly his birth, although it certainly was not as described in this article.

— Robert Briscoe, speaking for the anti-Treaty Republicans in Faneuil Hall, Boston, early 1923, quoted in his *For the Life of Me*

'Twas not a plot of cabbage green
(*Says the Shan Van Vocht*),
Nor a German submarine
(*Says the Shan Van Vocht*),
No, 'twas started down in Clare
By a man from God knows where—
So the people all declare
(*Says the Shan Van Vocht*).

—anonymous verse added to old folk-song
(1918)

General Sir Nevil Macready had disliked the Irish long before he was gazetted GOC-in-C, Ireland, in 1920: it was a time when racial and ethnic antipathies were counted virtuous, though not obligatory, in the higher ranks of military and civil society. The Irish historical gospel which would later sustain the priest-kingship of de Valera liked to imply that such things were the norm, indeed the rule, but in fact they varied greatly from officer to officer among the British troops in Ireland. What racial feeling existed, very often took the form of condescension, not unmixed with amusement, but for Macready it was full-hearted dislike. He wrote his *Annals of an Active Life* shortly after his retirement in 1923, and as de Valera was then at the lowest point of his fortunes since his entry into public life, Macready had neither motive nor inclination to say a kind word for 'this half-breed Spaniard'. But the time of writing gives a freedom to the portrait which no other time would permit for over half a century. It never seemed less necessary that a writer should take out literary insurance against a future prominence for de Valera in Anglo-Irish relations. So Macready could remove his elegant gloves in this case, where considerations of future British interests invited some civility on his part towards those Irish who, unlike de Valera, had accepted the Anglo-Irish Treaty of 1922.

De Valera and Macready met at the Mansion House, Dublin, in July 1921, after two years of bitter fighting between British and Irish forces. The meeting was to clear up preliminaries before full-scale negotiations between the President of the Irish Republic and the British Prime Minister (of whom, politically, and no doubt racially, Macready did not approve very much either). The real work to be done here by Macready was observation:

> From the moment I sat down next to him I saw that he was play-acting. He was evidently intent on impressing his audience with his importance and businesslike methods. He picked up little insignificant trifles, discussing them as if they were of paramount importance, all the time fidgeting with a pencil or scribbling away on the paper in front of him. Three times while I was there he hurriedly got up and left the room with short, quick steps for no apparent reason, and solely I believe to impress the rest of us with the idea of the weight of responsibility on his shoulders. It would be interesting to know what he did when he got outside: my own belief is—nothing. The impression I took away of him was that of a highly strung, vain individual of limited outlook, incapable of a broad view on any subject, but an adept at splitting hairs. Future events proved that he was deficient even in physical courage.

It is all very ungenerous, and it reveals the very limited imagination of the writer. Macready's definition of physical courage would have been crude. De Valera's three departures bear obvious explanations: Macready had been responsible for the deaths of many of de Valera's followers, and if these negotiations were to break down he might well be responsible for de Valera's own death. The departures could well be psychological devices to mask revulsion from the man of blood, together with natural physical responses to the tension of the situation. What probably happened was that on each occasion de Valera went to the lavatory, and very understandably too. But the overall impression merits respect. Macready knew what he meant by 'play-acting'. He was the son of the great Victorian actor, William Charles Macready.

We may discard Macready's assumptions as to de Valera's motivation— 'one who would always play to the gallery and lose himself in a maze of insignificant detail, not altogether uninfluenced by fears for his personal safety'.[1] De Valera was anxious to portray himself as the man of mind, the scholar, the teacher, distancing himself from the soldier, anxious to show Macready it was not a matter of one gunman being faced by another. But behind this obvious reasoning was something deeper. De Valera was not only acting this part, he was by the circumstances of his whole life a 'play-actor'. In fact, his background had made 'play-acting' as much of an occupational necessity as it had been for William Charles Macready, if he were to survive. The circumstances of his birth and upbringing had given him a reality he had to unlive. The story is tragic, and while de Valera's playing to the gallery knew all about the business of bidding for sympathy, he never bade for sympathy on this. He faced life from the start desperately alone and vulnerable, and he had every motive for focusing attention on *minutiae,* on performance and on ideology. From the beginning he had the best of all reasons for trusting nobody. His early life was overshadowed by the unspeakable grief of having been rejected by his own mother.

Kate Coll, of Bruree, co. Limerick, emigrated to the United States in 1879. She was 22. Her father, an agricultural labourer, had died in 1874. She was the eldest of four children. She followed the example of many Irish girls of labourer stock in seeking domestic service in New York. After two years she married, on 19 September 1881. Her husband, Vivion Juan de Valera, was a Spanish immigrant working as a music-teacher. Their son, Edward, was born in New York Nursery and Child Hospital, Lexington Avenue, on 14 October 1882. Two years later Vivion de Valera left his wife and child, supposedly in the interest of his health. He is reported as having died the next year. His wife went back to work. Their son was sent back to the agricultural labourer's cottage in Bruree with her brother Edward. There he lived with his grandmother—not yet fifty—his uncle Patrick, and his aunt Hannah. His mother made a brief visit to Bruree the following year and then returned to the United States, where she married again, this time to an Englishman, Charles Wheelwright. She refused to take her son to live with them, although he was still hoping that she would as late as 1896, when he wrote trying to get his Aunt Hannah (now also in the United States) to persuade her. She had a son by her second marriage, Thomas Wheelwright. The son of her first was known in Bruree as Eddie Coll.[2]

There seems to have been in Kate Coll a determined attempt to escape from her Irish background: two non-Irish marriages are noteworthy. It did not mean an attempt to escape from her native Roman Catholicism: her second son became a priest in the Redemptorist order, famous in Ireland for its hell-fire preaching. Her mother, who would bring up the infant de Valera, was herself a product of the complex network of migrant departure and return, having been born in England, so that in strict terms de Valera had but one Irish grandparent. But her family, the Carrolls, had been Irish and although seven of her eight siblings died in England, her father returned to Ireland to die after falling from a building on which he had been employed. Elisabeth Coll must have found life a hard enough struggle after the death of her husband when her eldest was seventeen and her youngest four. The agricultural labourers were the lowest caste in Irish society, and while folklore popularized the struggles of the tenant-farmers, immediately above them, it was the labourers who accounted for the highest death-tolls in time of famine. The conditions of 1879–81 came very near those of famine: a widespread loss of life was only prevented by extensive private charity, mostly American. Emigration and the hope of remittances from the departed children became the greatest means of salvation for families such as the Colls, whence the exiles of Kate and then her brother Edward to America. But Edward returned, bringing with him one more mouth to feed in the shape of his nephew and namesake. It is hardly surprising that Elisabeth Coll should have died in 1895, before she reached 60. Hannah had emigrated by then, and when Edward de Valera wrote to her in the desperate expedient of using her intercession to arouse her sister's maternal feelings, his specific reason was that his only remaining relative in the house, Uncle Pat, was about to get married. Young Eddie had made one close friend and he was leaving the area. It was the heart-cry of a boy with no person to call his own.

The terrible irony of this situation was that while De Valera was not illegitimate, his social circumstances left a strong presumption of illegitimacy. Social historians—misled by the language of respectability which the poor Irish Catholics took care to employ before officialdom, lay and clerical—have assumed from bureaucratic evidence that unmarried mothers were treated as outcasts and their children shunned. In practice it is clear that this was really not the case. The official existence of a stigma, however, was bad enough, even if it much outweighed the actuality. Abuse in playground fights could be quick enough to produce such suspicions in the ugliest form. And an unwanted love-child sent back from that land of temptation, the big American city, was not unusual, nor would be its maintenance with its grandmother should its mother actually succeed in getting married. What would be much more unusual would be the spectacle of a legitimate child excluded from its mother's second family. De Valera's authorized biography remarks that the young boy 'fought many a battle by the pump at the Bruree crossroads'—and it was no mere matter of fisticuffs. 'The loose stones which filled the pot-holes were telling ammunition.' The reason assigned for this in the book is that his uncle Pat used to be casually known as 'the Dane Coll'. This apparently arose because Pat Coll used to give out the rosary in chapel and was sarcastically referred to as the 'Dean', (pronounced locally as 'Dane'), presumably because of the punctilio with which he did it. But, recalled de Valera for his biographer T.P. O'Neill, the nephew had resented it as it seemed to imply his uncle was descended from the Norse invaders of early medieval Ireland. Combat for archaic reasons of Irish history was the kind of phenomenon de Valera liked to flaunt before British interlocutors (such as, when they finally met for negotiation, Lloyd George). But it is more likely that the stones were thrown to avenge his mother's name rather than his uncle's. Had his mother reclaimed him it would have effectively offset the misery he had suffered; it would have been a visible vindication. But she did not. Small wonder that he painstakingly recorded in the Bible he won as a prize in Blackrock College, in his late 'teens, any facts he could discover about his father.[3] The note was evidently added to: a correction about his father's place of death (Denver) is one such addition. There is touching self-identification in it: his sight was weak, and he notes the same in his father with the detail that it followed an accident, ending his training in sculpture. He was tall: his father was short. Mathematical himself, he carefully recorded his father's profession in music. The early information would have been from his relatives, not his mother, and the doubt about his father's place of death could mean that Vivion de Valera abandoned his wife and child. (She would have been obliged to find proof of his death when marrying Wheelwright.) It was all so unreal to him that he even noted his father's being fluent in his own native language, Spanish, as well as German, English and French. And it is urgent: in defiance of the old and bitter memories of schoolboy insult, he was carefully accumulating detail as to his father's existence.

His authorized biographer makes one comment at the close of his book which, like the rest, would have required de Valera's permission and which in the place where it appears looks like the opinion he himself wanted to leave with posterity:

> An Irish immigrant mother—a Spanish-American father dying while he was very small—a return to Ireland, his mother remaining in America—an upbringing by an uncle in what he himself has called a labourer's cottage—no psychiatrist could forecast the outcome of such an inheritance and early environment. The President never tired of expressing his gratefulness to his grandmother and his uncle Pat, but from his earliest years, without father or mother to guide him, he had to fend for himself compared with others. One cannot say what effect this must have had on a small boy's formation. In fact, he grew up with a strong confidence in himself, powerful family affection and a surpassing love of Ireland.[4]

There can be no question about the powerful family affection: de Valera became a devoted—if often absent—husband and father. But it is unrelated to those who brought him up. The only names from his own background he bestowed on his children were those of his father and himself. He was dutifully grateful to Uncle Pat, but for all of its patriotic

connotations his was not one of the names bestowed on de Valera's sons. It
is de Valera's recollection that speaks in his authorized biography:

> Uncle Pat was quite severe with his nephew; he disapproved of wasting time
> with such games as hurling. He thrashed Eddie when he went 'on the slinge'
> (played truant) or, as he did once, used the donkey's Sunday pair of reins to
> make a swing.[5]

And after marriage Patrick Coll fades out of the story. The 'surpassing
love of Ireland' can be reasonably seen as compensation for the lack of any
permanent family and the rejection by his mother; suffice it to say for the
present that it involved a massive self-identification. Ireland became the
mother whom he so constituted in his own mind that she would never
betray him, whatever some of her undutiful progeny might do at the polls.
And as for the 'strong confidence in himself', he really had no alternatives.

De Valera's discovery of Ireland in the form that he found it would have
been deeply related to the one major figure in Irish history whom he knew
in his childhood. Significantly, it was his parish priest, a figure of
international celebrity and of impeccable patriotism.[6] The Revd Eugene
Sheehy was known as 'the Land League priest'; but for all of that famous
agrarian movement's glorification of the tenant farmer, the waif from the
labourer's cottage was given the privilege of becoming an altar-boy when
there would have been high competition for such an honour. This must
have been very important to the boy: somebody wanted him. Sheehy's
great-nephew, the late Owen Sheehy-Skeffington, told me that Father
Eugene, so far as he could gather, would have made an excellent parent,
adding wickedly that his own grandfather, David Sheehy, MP, would have
been ideally suited for the priesthood. (Owen was a vigorously anti-clerical
agnostic.) De Valera may have benefited from the paternal instincts; he
certainly hungered for them.

Sheehy had been imprisoned in Kilmainham Gaol in 1881 under the
Coercion Act which enabled the Gladstone administration to incarcerate
malcontents against whom a jury trial was presumed useless. It is an
indication as to how much anxiety Sheehy had created that the government
went to the extreme of throwing a priest into jail almost as soon as they
obtained the legal power. Eventually he had to be released on the grounds
of health, and was then sent to the United States to raise money for the
Land League. Persistent rumours linked him with the surviving Fenians in
the United States, and there is strong evidence that he belonged to one of
the Fenian organizations but was, if so, of the section of that group of

sworn supporters of an Irish Republic which believed in working through the land agitation and its links with the Parliamentary Party under Parnell. On his return Sheehy had to fight his own suspension from the priesthood by his bishop, Edward Thomas O'Dwyer of Limerick, exceptional among the Catholic hierarchy in his hatred for the Land League. Appeal to Rome was necessary for his reinstatement, and he had to fulfil his part of the bargain by confining himself to his new parish, Bruree. It may well be imagined how much his frustration worked itself out by means of patriotic sermons on suitable occasions. It is said that when Catholics were given a Papal dispensation from Friday abstinence from meat on the occasion of Queen Victoria's Jubilee, Father Sheehy so informed his congregation with the additional remark 'but as for me, it would stick in my throat and choke me'. One might expect, also, that he would have given his altar-server some account of the death of his collateral ancestor, Father Nicholas Sheehy, who had been hanged in Clonmel in 1766 for a murder of which he had been convicted on perjured evidence. Father Nicholas Sheehy was likewise suspected of implication in agrarian conspiracy. And many of these powerful consecrations of faith in Irish freedom were delivered in the heart of the Mass, with the boy whom he had taken from his obscure and despised location sitting at his feet before the entire congregation, an essential figure in the religious ritual and no less enthusiastic a votary of the patriotic which from time to time accompanied it. The great mind and inspiration of Eugene Sheehy would seem the first direct influence shaping de Valera for his future priest-kingship.

Father Sheehy's quietude after his controversy with the Bishop kept him officially out of public agitation. In any case, he had been critical of Parnell's moderation before his (and during Sheehy's) imprisonment in 1881, and privately probably became so once more after the Land League's dissolution the following year. Sheehy certainly encouraged hurling in the parish, and de Valera's clash with his uncle over the unprofitable cause of Gaelic games sounds like the parish priest's influence at work. After de Valera had gone to boarding-school and college, in Dublin, Sheehy became active in 1904 in encouraging a national monument to the memory of Theobald Wolfe Tone, French Revolutionary sympathizer, leader of the United Irishmen and reputed modern founder of the gospel of Irish separatism. If Tone's atheism, secularism and suicide did not stand in Sheehy's way, why should his former altar-boy hang back? Tone's name was joined in the proposed honours with those of his revolutionary colleague Lord Edward Fitzgerald, and with the Young Ireland journalist and nationalist ideologue Thomas Davis. Father Sheehy also organized a

Gaelic League branch in his parish around the same time; de Valera joined the Gaelic League in 1908.[7]

There was at least one practical manifestation of the secular spirit of Father Sheehy in the childhood of de Valera. He told T.P. O'Neill of seeing a meeting organized in the village to inaugurate the boycott of a local landowner and horse-breeder. It was an instructive lesson in the marshalling of community spirit to wield the weapon of ostracism. It was a distinctly two-edged sword. On the one hand, it held the people to a gospel of non-violent protest, and could be very effective, as had been shown in its initial exhibition against the land agent who involuntarily gave the practice its name, Captain Charles S. Boycott. On the other, it could be a cruel method of instilling a rigid conformity, and in some variants spread far beyond its initial purpose of protecting tenants against arbitrary eviction and landlord oppression. De Valera's chief recollection was that of 'the biggest drum he had ever seen'; he 'never forgot the pomp and glory which that drum represented for him'. The recollection does not seem to have included the thought that the use of the drum for purposes of community solidarity had probably been copied from the Orangemen of Ulster. Or perhaps it did, and if so it was with approval for the idea of the South taking up the Northern weapon.

This episode seems to have taken place when de Valera was very small: he remembered seeing the drum when he was standing in petticoats looking from an attic window. His later memories included being told to graze cows for his uncle illegally—there was little land attached to the labourer's cottage—and keeping one eye out for the police. This supplied a practical sense of civil disaffection to support the lessons in revolutionary nationalism being administered piecemeal by Father Sheehy. But if there was little to inculcate respect for state authority, his grandmother was emphatic about breeding in him a sense of devotion to the Church. Even before Father Sheehy brought him to the forefront of observance, Elisabeth Coll had been in the habit of solving the baby-sitting problem by parking him alone in the church while she went around Bruree. 'I was lonely', he told her, revealingly, when she asked how he got on. 'How could you be lonely in God's house? Why didn't you talk to Him?' His recollection would seem to imply that he followed the direction. For all of its political implications, the religious basis to the practice should not be slighted. He continued to talk to God, alone, for the rest of his life; it does not detract from his sincerity to say that he did it without fear of much contradiction. The practice would have reinforced another lesson he drew from Father Sheehy—that private opinions might be held on questions of nationalism despite the hostility of established ecclesiastical authority. The emphasis on Catholics being bound by an 'informed conscience' was a doctrine which only became fashionable when de Valera had formally retired from active politics, but his grandmother had involuntarily ensured that he would practice it all of his life, and Father Sheehy gave him that with which to inform it.

He received education at the national primary school in Bruree, from time to time interrupted by his household obligations. (He seems to have become Uncle Pat's cook when his grandmother died, until the postponed awakening of Uncle Pat's amatory sensibilities turned him to more orthodox means of culinary support.) He went on to secondary education with the Christian Brothers in Charleville, walking the seven miles. In default of a return to America, it was his only chance to break out of Bruree, and he threw himself into the Greek and Latin, English and French and—what would become a lifelong passion—mathematics. Mathematics was, fundamentally, a reliable science: de Valera's had been a very unreliable world. His enthusiasm for it indicates a love of order and a desire for its inculcation; but it was no abstract parrot-cry with him. He ultimately won an exhibition to Blackrock College, in Dublin, which effectively ended his dependence on his Bruree relatives, and on Bruree itself. But it was not a mere matter of romanticization of his past which subsequently led him to a Jeffersonian style of ideological leadership in praise of rural society. He really believed that, for all of his loneliness, he had found virtue in the rural life. After all, if Bruree had been unable to provide real substitutes for his lost parents, it had given him the means of making something of his own life, much more indeed than appeared at the outset. He never forgot it. He would be ridiculed by sophisticated opponents for his open admiration for the country, and was sneered at by the *Irish Times* for preaching a 'Gaelic-speaking, potato-digging Republic'. But to the end he proudly noted his hold on the rural vote.

The negative aspects of his life affected his subsequent career in a different way. His Constitution of 1937 would make much of the sacred nature of the family, and preach the ideal of woman's place in the home. It conflicted oddly with the spirit of the Sinn Féin movement which had brought him to the forefront. Ireland is traditionally seen as peculiarly reactionary in the sphere of women's rights. Yet women played a formidable part in the winning and making of the new state. Women staffed many of the major posts in the National University of Ireland of which he became Chancellor in 1921; women supported the drive of the Socialist movement, the artistic Renaissance, the nationalist cause. The

cause of Irish female suffrage fuelled many allied crusades. De Valera's
Constitution defied that. He had headed the Sinn Féin candidates in the
election of 1918 including Constance Markiewicz, the first woman elected
to the House of Commons though not taking her seat, but his own party,
Fianna Fáil, was decidedly backward in the furtherance of that tradition.
He did not take the principle to extremes in personal terms: his daughter
Máirín ultimately became Professor of Botany in University College
Galway. But his record after 1932 was an anti-feminist one, and this is
directly to be ascribed to his personal sorrow at the loss of a family life. He
told himself, in telling others, that his failure to be reunited with his mother
was due to her being forced into the sordid world of employment at the
expense of her fulfilment of family obligations. He saw himself as having a
mission to prevent other such tragedies for children in the future. This was
perhaps the clearest public manifestation of his awareness of a lost
childhood. Its other effects were much more deep-rooted, and less capable
of directly expressing themselves.

De Valera was not a Gandhi, although certain aspects of Gandhi's irony,
asceticism and courage in placing Indian nationalism above British,
whatever the temptation, would have appealed to him; he was himself
more of a Nehru. But he was a Nehru from a caste which was untouchable,
and a birth which seemed worse. Macaulay (whom de Valera read as a boy)
testifies to the role of the Roman Catholic Church in the medieval world as
a force which enabled the poorest to rise to the top in specific cases: he cited
the English beggar, Nicholas Breakspear, who became a Pope, Adrian IV,
and whose Bull *Laudabiliter* bestowed Ireland on Henry II. The Church
played a similar role for de Valera, first through Father Sheehy, then
through the Holy Ghost Fathers at Blackrock College. It did not do so in its
usual way, that of the priesthood. De Valera apparently thought of
becoming a priest about the age of 16, and the Holy Ghosts were impressed
with his academic record, but suggested that he choose their lay College
rather than their Scholasticate, although they sent the Prospectus of the
latter to him. It was a wise precaution to test the strength of his vocation; it
may also indicate that they were not too precipitate in pushing labourers'
children for ordination. But they were very welcoming. His local curate,
Father Liston, had used a personal acquaintance with the President of
Blackrock to further the boy's claims, and the President, Father Lawrence
Healy, CSSp, noted that 'If his application is equal to his proved talents he
ought to have a pretty brilliant career both in the Intermediate and at the
Royal University'. So de Valera was rescued, although in the process he
lost touch with his caste.

Where his labourer origins would surface in his political life was again in negative terms: for all of his talk of the country, and his followers' insistence that the farmers were the backbone of the country, de Valera did not like the 'strong farmers' who had profited so well from the Land League and its ultimate consequences of enablement of tenant purchase of holdings, and the 'strong farmers' did not like him. Bernard Shaw's *John Bull's Other Island,* written while de Valera was in Blackrock, conveys the utter contempt in which the ambitious and newly emancipated farmers held the labourers and their possible economic advancement ('hwat man in his senses ever wanted to give land to Patsy Farll an dhe like o him?'). The nearest de Valera came to identification with his own people was in the alliance he built up with the small farmers, who could not afford the social pretensions of their more fortunate colleagues.

De Valera's idealization of the Bruree of his childhood depended on memory, for he never lived in the country again apart from boarding-school teaching at Rockwell, electoral activities, and military exigencies. But it was greatly deepened and strengthened by *Knocknagow,* the famous novel written by Charles Kickham shortly after his release from prison in 1869 after four years' hard servitude for Fenian activities. Kickham, for most of his life partially blind and deaf, came from south Tipperary, which borders on de Valera's Limerick, and died in Blackrock, near the College, in the year of de Valera's birth. The book is highly derivative of Dickens and George Eliot, but it inveighs against a modernizing world which destroys a community much as Goldsmith posits in 'The Deserted Village'. (It is perhaps necessary to advise a British audience that Kickham, like most of Goldsmith's Irish Catholic readers, would have assumed the subject of that poem to be Irish.) Kickham's biographer, R.V. Comerford, describes de Valera's St Patrick's Day broadcast of 1943 as 'virtually paraphrasing *Knocknagow* for people whom he knew to be imbued with its sentiments'.[8] De Valera, in the midst of the Second World War, declared:

> Acutely conscious though we all are of the misery and desolation in which the greater part of the world is plunged, let us turn aside for the moment to that ideal Ireland that we would have. That Ireland which we dreamed of would be the home of a people who valued material wealth only as the basis of right living, of a people who were satisfied with frugal comfort and devoted their leisure to the things of the spirit—a land whose countryside would be bright with cosy homesteads, whose fields and villages would be joyous with the sounds of industry, with the romping of sturdy children, the contests of

athletic youths and the laughter of comely maidens, whose firesides would be forums for the wisdom of serene old age. It would, in a word, be the home of a people living the life that God desires that man should live.

But while de Valera knew he was appealing to the still vigorous readership of *Knocknagow,* the conviction is unmistakable. On the other hand, there is play-acting in it, although the actor has to tell himself that the play is reality. He liked to imagine that he was speaking of a potential Ireland of the future, and to imply that in certain respects it was the Ireland in which he passed his early youth, but his imagery came from a novel published before his own birth, extolling a situation supposedly existing years before the time of writing, and itself drawn from a poem written a century before the novel's composition in which the lost Golden Age is based on perceptions decades anterior to that. Goldsmith's vision of the village before desertion, insofar as it had Irish antecedents at all, derived from phenomena exactly 200 years before de Valera's broadcast. A more striking example of nostalgic agrarian populism could hardly be found.

To add to the ironies, the condition of the Irish Catholics in 1743 was in social and political terms the worst in history: they were the uttermost in degradation, and the law, in the famous words of a judge on the bench, did not presume such a thing as an Irish Roman Catholic to exist. That memory was retained with great bitterness among Irish Catholics; yet it could coexist insensible of self-contradiction, with the image of a lost rural Paradise. Kickham, indeed, had struggled for the independence of an Irish Republic while rigidly opposing any attempts to alter the land system, and to the end of his days ferociously opposed Fenian or (to give the movement the name it bore in Ireland) Irish Republican Brotherhood support of Parnell's constitutionalism or the Land League. There might be bad landlords: but the ideal was good ones. The Land League was nevertheless the cause of all but a tiny minority of Irish nationalists by the time he died: yet Kickham exacted his tribute. Father Eugene Sheehy, speaking for the Land League in Chicago on 2 December 1881, declared 'We wish to destroy landlordism only as the stepping-stone to a greater and higher end.' Although Kickham had condemned all legislation inimical to landlordism, the principles came to be that the war on landlordism was intended to realize the ideals of Kickham. The success of Kickham's gospel as an agrarian ideal was, in part, based on a concept of national identity across class lines, for all that those lines had been eloquently and lucidly perceived in his novel. And there was the fact that his hero, Mat the Thrasher, was a labourer, the most lovable and most heroic literary vision of an Irish labourer ever achieved. De Valera had to act the part of prophet of a Kickhamite Ireland, for it was in its social cohesion, not in the reality of social conflict, that his own class representative, with whom he could identify, had found his apotheosis.

Knocknagow meant a symbolical acceptance for de Valera by Ireland, and it was important that the author whose work realized that ideal had been an intransigent Republican. This did not mean that de Valera was a youthful Republican, but Father Sheehy may have made him an infant one—a memory to be revived, after many years' lapse, in the second decade of the new century. Kickham's immediate effect was to give an important reactionary caste to de Valera's agrarian thought. He would find in the thought of Patrick Pearse, as he grew to foster his posthumous cult, much that echoed such attitudes. This did not imply a desire to repeal the land legislation of Gladstone and later of the Tories, or to follow Kickham's regret at the success of Parnell; it simply enjoyed the luxury of demanding a new world on premises envisioned by the old. Even de Valera's ritualistic rhetoric of 1943 gave the clue to the old, half-lost contours of the Kickhamite ideal: 'athletic youths' and 'comely maidens' were archaic terms by the time of his boyhood, let alone 1943. In part, this strange Latinate world of vocabulary which he came to inhabit derived from his training by the Holy Ghost Fathers, whose daily obligation of Latin prayer and service made such English natural to them and to the pupil whose vindication of their hopes for him was so vital to his survival. He would also draw from them another form of alienation from the state: the simple faith that the Holy Ghost Fathers and their fellow-priests knew far better the needs of a just society than did the parliament or government of the United Kingdom of Great Britain and Ireland.

The habits of thrift and frugality practised by de Valera all his life were thrust on him from the first, and Dublin in 1898 made little change in this. His daily pilgrimage to the school in Charleville had won him his freedom by gaining him an exhibition for £20, which the President of Blackrock, Father Laurence Healy, accepted in lieu of the normal fee of £40. But before the boy could achieve his freedom, there was a wrangle from Uncle Patrick Coll who tried to get £5 of the exhibition from the Holy Ghosts; they simply ignored him. Again to quote Father Sheehy in Chicago (and no doubt Bruree) 'Nothing good—nothing great has been purchased without sacrifice. No birth—above all that of Freedom—has been without pain'. The physical asceticism of de Valera had to be matched by a psychological asceticism. A suit of clothes had somehow to be squeezed out of sparse funds, and de Valera with difficulty found his way to the new school, where his loneliness was somewhat alleviated by his first encounter, for Brother McGrath had a Tipperary accent. On the other hand, the first master of whom he fell foul was also the first Ulsterman he had ever met. For all of his formal hostility to the partition of Ireland in future years, his sense of that province as alien never seems to have left him. He professed no surprise when he discovered that master had afterwards supported the Anglo-Irish Treaty he denounced.

De Valera performed well as a student and continued to give thought to the idea of becoming a missionary priest; but he received little encouragement. He showed particular proficiency in Christian Doctrine in which he defeated for First Place the future Cardinal Archbishop of Armagh, John D'Alton. This pleasing symbolism of his perpetual assurance of theological orthodoxy had some significance by the time of his formal entry into Irish nationalist politics, in 1913, for by then D'Alton was already a Maynooth Professor. De Valera seems to have been very attached to his rival, and in a letter to his unknown half-brother Wheelwright praised D'Alton's defeat of him in Classics, rather than his own success. But he never showed signs of a spiritual inferiority complex thereafter. It was not until his second year that de Valera made his first really close friendship since Bruree—with Frank Hughes of Mayo, two years his senior. He was brought to the Hugheses for Christmas in Kiltimagh in 1899, and an ornamental greeting in highly elaborate script survives from de Valera to Hughes

When the evening sun is sinking
And your mind from trouble free,
When of absent friends you're thinking
Don't forget to think of me.

It is under the inscription 'In memoriam amici tui et in aeternum, Edward de Valera 1899/1900'. The sentiment may be banal, but the gentle hunger for friendship it records is heartrending. The boy from Bruree only ventures to ask a very humble place in the recollection of his own dearest friend.

De Valera continued to gain good Honours in Blackrock, winning the needful Exhibitions to maintain himself there. The College had been affiliated to the Royal University of Ireland such that de Valera was able to continue there as a student in training for a University degree with the advantage of preserving the sense of identity with the Holy Ghost institution he had been building up. He matriculated for the University, winning tenth place in Ireland. He was to study his beloved Mathematics, and the Holy Ghosts found him a tutor who had been a student at their Tipperary school, Rockwell College, Cashel. His name was Michael Smithwick, and when he presented de Valera with a mathematical copy book, the boy noted the curious fact that the signature was a gallant attempt to write the name in Irish—Micheál Smidic. De Valera had been aware of signs of a growing fad for Irish; but his economic needs gave him little opportunity for indulgence in such an obvious luxury and he did nothing about it now. But he may have met a schoolmate of Smithwick's who visited Blackrock, from St Kieran's, Kilkenny, where he was now teaching, to play Rugby, a game of which de Valera had become very fond. Smithwick's friend, Thomas MacDonagh, arrived armed with a copy of his first book of poems, which he presented to the President of Blackrock, now Father John T. Murphy. MacDonagh was also a Tipperary man, from Cloughjordan near Nenagh, not far from the borders of Clare where in 1917 de Valera would win his first Parliamentary election. But in addition to Rugby de Valera was generally blossoming out as an athlete, throwing himself into cricket, boxing, handball, hurling and javelin throwing. He became a noted runner and cyclist, and a debater who spoke 'a little in favour of both' free trade and protection, and firmly espoused constitutional monarchy against republicanism. He evidently equated republicanism with democracy, and expressed disapproval of both with the words, 'There is no rule so tyrannical as that of them all.' He showed hankerings towards the age of chivalry, but later reversed himself to speak well of the abolition of serfdom and call for the spread of education to all. On the other hand his detailed paper on the University question argued for a Catholic College in Dublin University which had but one, Protestant, college, Trinity, and doubted whether the Belfast Presbyterians were sufficiently advanced for a University (regardless of the fact that they had a flourishing college of the Queen's University). Eventually, in 1903, de Valera was persuaded to apply for a teaching post at Rockwell—which he obtained—after completing his Second Arts examination. His sponsors included one of the Blackrock professors (as they were styled in conformity with the Royal University affiliation): John Haugh, who had been a close friend of Kickham.

De Valera settled in at Rockwell, and made friends with the other lay masters, one of whom trained him in drilling and military tactics. Another, Tom O'Donnell, began the lifelong fashion of addressing him as 'Dev'. He played the bombardon with the College orchestra; he played Rugby with mixed results; he played the gallant with the daughter of a hotel proprietor. But the year set back his work for his degree, and after a summer's study at

Blackrock he had to be content with a Pass rather than an Honours. He finally decided against the priesthood. He put in another year at Rockwell. Again, he must have heard talk of Thomas MacDonagh who had completed a period of study and teaching there before his arrival and published his second volume of poems with a dedication to the Rockwell Dean of Studies. De Valera decided to look for post-graduate work in Mathematics combined with some teaching, and found a place in the Dublin Jesuit school, Belvedere. Thence he took a post in Carysfoot Training College for teachers. He was still there in 1908 when in the words of Father Seán P. Farragher in his invaluable *Dev and his Alma Mater* he 'fell in love with the Irish language and his Irish teacher', Sinéad Ni Fhlannagáin (Janet Flanagan).

De Valera maintained throughout his life the closest reserve about his family background: legends proliferated, and he made little attempt to contradict any that were favourable. Sinéad, who married him in 1910, naturally co-operated in this by strong shyness. But some things are clear. She was an exceptionally noble woman. She had a genuine simplicity of character which placed a great value on human goodness and kindness. She showed heroic fortitude in her efforts to save her husband's life in 1916 and provide for their family in the desperate poverty created by his subsequent imprisonment. She was a devoted mother, and carried on that work for grandchildren who were left motherless. She was not political. She gave her husband the love of which he had been starved.

She was de Valera's senior by over four years. She was born in Balbriggan, co. Dublin, in a bourgeois family which, like herself, stayed out of the limelight thereafter. One cousin, Laurence, had been at Blackrock at the same time as de Valera; with another, Tom, a dentist, he seems to have been on terms as friendly as it is possible to be with one's dentist. Yet for all of her shyness her intellectual interests had brought her into the heady waters of the Irish Renaissance where de Valera, as Seán Ó Faoláin has put it, 'led . . . what can only be called a very compressed life . . . in a city then far from provincial . . . what can only be called a somewhat provincial life. . . He has remained, all his life long, infected by his youthful provincialism.'[9] Sinéad saw much of the Gaelic League, and a little of the theatre. She had discussed the possibility of a theatrical career with the most repulsive and wittiest aesthete of the Irish Renaissance, George Moore. She had performed in a play by Douglas Hyde. She charmed Seán O'Casey. She ultimately became an accomplished writer of children's fairy stories in Irish. She translated with elegance from the French, and remained conversant with significant developments in music.

She was an inspired teacher of Irish under the auspices of the Gaelic League, teaching in the Connacht dialect in what was called the Leinster College. It was there that she discovered to de Valera a whole new identity. Thomas MacDonagh in his *Literature in Ireland* (itself one of the great seminal books of the Irish Renaissance) said that 'All of us find in Irish rather than in English a satisfying understanding of certain ways of ours and the best expression of certain of our emotions.' It struck deeper, psychologically, than English; it offered more basic identity. It also offered the means of stretching the mind, particularly in terms of subtlety and beauty. It is the language of the grace note, the nuance, the emotion as soft as its gutterals and aspirates. It transformed de Valera's sense of Irishness. He had been in search of aesthetics, even in so unlikely a field of mathematics, and his failure to reach Honours in his primary degree had been partly caused by his fascination with its newly-developing philosophy. His growing sense of Irishness had led him to pursue a particularly Irish contribution to the science, Sir William Rowan Hamilton's theory of quaternions: again, he sought the future by rekindling an ancient fire. But Irish offered a new world, a fairy landscape, alongside the remorseless logic of mathematics. Its highly democratic forms of speech, and its classes where teaching and learning went on among all ages, transformed his associations with his fellows from the hierarchical gradations in education he had known up to now. He might find himself being corrected by a schoolboy as well as a greybeard. He discovered the beauty of being taught by a teacher with whom one is in love.

Sinéad's Irish was beautiful, but it was not complex. It is probable that de Valera found his wife and his Irish most appealing in their simplicity. The world was subtle and devious, and he himself would learn that art of taking refuge in subtleties for concealment of intent and maximization of alternatives. Irish might be subtle, but it was not a language for concealment, not as Sinéad talked it anyway. Fundamentally, Irish for de Valera himself was an escape to the golden world of love his wife had opened for him. His conviction as to its necessity for a true self-realization of Irish nationhood was deeply sincere, but because it was so much associated with private happiness for him, he could never find the means of conveying its true implications for him. In matters of ritual, it served his needs. He found the appropriate formulae, much as he had known their Latin equivalents when he had been an altar-boy. But original political thought did not come to him in Irish: it was his language to affirm and renew his beliefs, not to discover the magnitude of their ramifications. He

put it very well on 14 December 1921 at the commencement of the debate on
the Treaty which to his extreme displeasure Collins, Griffith and their
fellows had brought back from Lloyd George:

> *Tá fhios againn go léir cé an fáth go bhfuilimíd anso iniu agus an cheist mhór
> atá againn le socrú. Níl mo chuid Gaedhilge chó maith agus ba mhaith liom í
> bheith. Is fearr is féidir liom mo smaointe do nochtadh as Beurla, agus dá
> bhrí sin is dóich liom gurbh fhearra dhom labhairt as Beurla ar fad.* Some of
> the members do not know Irish, I think, and consequently what I shall say
> will be in English.

But that last sentence was not what he had said in Irish, although it implied
that it was. What he had said in Irish was:

> We all know why we are here today with this great question we have to be
> settled. My share of Irish is not as good as I would like it to be. I can bare my
> thoughts better in English, and for that reason I think it is better for me to
> speak entirely in English.

Irish, therefore, remained for him a language in which to describe rather
than to conceptualize. But it also offered a means of privacy, appropriately
given its place in his very private marriage: and it was a means of solidifying
the tribe by intimation to Gaelic speakers of secret comunications to be
concealed from those ignorant of it. It was symbolic that his first action in
this vital debate was to distance those outside his charmed circle of Irish-
speakers, whatever their individual views on this question, by a deception:
but the deception itself was in English and what he said in Irish was frank to
the extent of confessional. He was' about to pronounce on titles to
nationality, and whether this Treaty did or did not impair them. Yet his
first action was to assert a limitation to his own infallibility in the very
matter of a foremost credential. There was also a symbol that what was
said to those ignorant of Irish enjoyed a lower level of truth than what was
said to those familiar with it. It is ironical that nobody thought that to
suggest an oath in English to the King, as prescribed by the Treaty, could be
comfortably regarded as less binding than an oath in Irish to the Republic.
But the implication is clear enough: English henceforth became, to put it
most politely, the language of diplomacy, where Irish invited frankness.
Irish was sacred: Irish was Sinéad. English had given him grief; Irish had
given him love.[10]

   But why, then, like Sinéad's future heroes and heroines in her Gaelic
fairy-stories did they not simply live happily ever after? They had found
a flat in Morehampton Road, Donnybrook, arboreal and quiet,

unpretentious and residential. They had their common interest in the Gaelic League. They had the Hugheses as good friends—Frank had married some months after the de Valera wedding in January 1910, and they had been one another's best men, and then godfathers to the first children. And indeed in spring 1911, the first had arrived in the shape of little Vivion: the lost Father, supplanted and forgotten, was now to be vindicated and commemorated in his grandson. There were problems, certainly. Even the altruistic pursuit of the ancestral sweet and kingly tongue could prove a thorny way: de Valera had found his new bicycle was stolen while he was searching a bookshop for the correct form of an Irish marriage service. Irish was winning him interesting new acquaintances—the passionate founder of the Gaelic League Douglas Hyde; the scholar transforming early Irish history, Eoin MacNeill; the world-famous diplomat and antislavery agitator Sir Roger Casement; the schoolmaster and Gaelic polemicist Patrick Pearse; and possibly Pearse's school colleague, Thomas MacDonagh. De Valera had also sealed his new identity in a new name: he was no longer Edward—a name of British connotations more disturbing to de Valera at the death of Edward VII than they had been at his accession in 1901—he was now 'Éamonn', which by the later 1920s would be refined to 'Éamon'. More correctly the name meant 'Edmund', so in a sense de Valera was now without a name in English. It did not immediately ease his acceptance: the Gaelic League newspaper, confused by his now general salutation as 'Dev', simply styled him 'Devalero'.

There was a more curious hiatus in his acceptance which disturbed him. He was proposed for the executive committee of the Gaelic League and was sure of acceptance. But he was mysteriously defeated, and sensed a conspiracy against him. It seemed political. The Gaelic League tended to make political nationalists of its votaries, even those of Unionist origin who had joined purely because of its cultural conservation. But de Valera, in 1911, like many of the major figures including Pearse, was then a Home Ruler. The Irish Parliamentary Party was principally concerned with Westminster political pressures and patronage. But it now held the balance of power, and the long-sought dream of legislature in Dublin seemed on the verge of success. De Valera was aware of a small, intransigently separatist party, Sinn Féin ('We Ourselves'), which, swayed by the impassioned and xenophobic journalism of Arthur Griffith, demanded a dual monarchy after the fashion of Austria-Hungary. Griffith was, among other unpleasing things, an anti-Semite, and de Valera may have concluded that the Sinn Féin element had manoeuvred against him because of suspected Jewish blood, a charge not new to him: the freedom of anti-Semitic attack on him in subsequent years confirmed him in his own dislike of anti-Semitism. For whatever reason, he was certain Sinn Féin was behind his defeat. In fact, whatever its malevolence, it had no such organizational capacity. His candidacy had been defeated because the newly reviving Irish Republican Brotherhood, consecrated to an exploitation of all the rising phenomena of Irish nationalism, pushed in its own man. He could thank a small, charming, intensely conspiratorial manipulator named Seán MacDermott, whose ruthlessness, deviousness and resourcefulness were matched by his inability to make any personal headway in the Irish language. He may have assisted in the nurturing of de Valera's rancour against Sinn Féin to divert his attentions from the real culprits, the IRB.

Soon there came a much more serious check from another quarter. De Valera had learned Connacht Irish, but it was his native Munster to which he sought a return when in 1913 he applied for the Professorship of Mathematical Physics in University College, Cork, one of the three constituent colleges of the newly-founded National University of Ireland. De Valera's title of professor at Carysfort was, as Ó Faoláin has put it, 'a trifle magniloquent'. He hankered for the real thing, but he only achieved it through the significant success of three of his children and one son-in-law winning professorial Chairs (often in the teeth of bitter academic hatred of himself). His credentials for Cork were weak; he had a Pass degree, he had never finished his post-graduate degree in Mathematical Physics. (His potential for the post was none the less good.) He worked industriously to gain the votes of county councillors on the Governing Body, employing such allies as prominent Gaelic Leaguers like the Kerry writer Patrick Sugrue (afterwards famous under the pseudonym *'An Seabhac'*), and the Cork Redmondite solicitor John Horgan (whom he easily convinced of his loyalty to the Irish Parliamentary Party). But, however gratifying his Gaelic credentials to Horgan and Sugrue, the College president, Sir Bertram Windle (late of Birmingham), had no intention of allowing the Chair of applied mathematics to be made a fief of insurgent linguistic nationalism. When de Valera tied first place at the Governing Body, every possible means of keeping him out was employed to turn the vote in the Senate of the entire University, which had the final say. He was obliterated. It was the victory of the old establishment over the new; it was also—whatever de Valera might think—the victory of professional standards over local influence.[11]

It was not entirely surprising that, in the larger context of Westminster, another old establishment now began to seem to de Valera as also likely to win an unexpected last-ditch victory over the new. The Unionists and

Tories were mobilizing against Home Rule. What they were no longer able to check by constitutional politics, they threatened to prevent by force. The Dublin Protestant barrister, Sir Edward Carson, threw his career aside to make the maximum use of Ulster Protestant intransigence, and mobilize its military potential. Under his auspices, Ulstermen and their Tory English supporters marched, covenanted, drilled and ultimately armed against the threatened legislation. Carson had started out as the Dublin Castle crown prosecutor, 'Coercion Carson', during the severe regime of Chief Secretary 'Bloody Balfour', and Irish nationalist opinion readily assumed Ulster was merely a pawn. The cynical phrase of Lord Randolph Churchill that 'the Orange card is the card to play' was nowhere more destructive in its effects than in Catholic Ireland: Protestant Ulster seemed not a people, but a stratagem. Carson, whose eyes were clearly on Dublin and London—he had hardly even been to Ulster before 1911—must surely be mobilizing in Ulster for an attack on the rest of Ireland. Reactions in the Catholic South were to assume that the Unionist show of force must be matched by a Home Rule show of force. Hence the Dublin response was formally derivative: the Irish Volunteers would deal with the Ulster Volunteers. In theory, there was little about this which diverged from pure Parnellism. The Parnell movement had in its rise relied on an extra-constitutional agitation, very often with the specific intent of answering Tory bullying in the Irish landed estates or in Westminster. Only a return to Parnell's policy of stiffening the backs of the government would call this bluff. Eoin MacNeill, the founder of the Volunteers, talked of the possibility of Carson marching to Cork. De Valera, writing a foreword to the Reverend Professor F.X. Martin's invaluable compilation *The Irish Volunteers 1913–1915* in 1963, isolated three main currents of thought as going in to the making of the Irish Volunteers:

> First, there were those who, seeing our people being robbed of the fruits of decades of patient constitutional endeavour by an arrogant defiance of constitution and law, simply wanted to counter force by force. The Manifesto made it clear that defensive and protective, not aggressive, action was intended, but if force could be used to prevent Home Rule then a greater force could be used to secure it. Those who felt thus, formed, I believe, no inconsiderable part of the recruits who flocked to the Volunteer standard the moment it was raised.
>
> Next, there were those who saw in the situation a heaven-sent opportunity to repair the mistake made when the Volunteer Organization of 1782 was allowed to lapse. The circumstances of 1913 made the creation of a similar

organization again possible, and this time it would not be allowed to lapse. It would be preserved as a guarantee of civil rights and national freedom.

Some of those who thought like this fondly hoped that, in view of their tradition, the Volunteers of the North would, one day, stand shoulder to shoulder with their brothers of the South in common defence of their motherland and of their liberties as freemen. They felt sure, moreover, that the English Tories and the feudal lords who instigated and directed the arming of the North would quickly learn that they had made a fundamental mistake in assuming that the rank and file, the 'wage earners and rent payers' of the North could be retained for long as subservient tools.

Finally, there were those whose thought went deeper and was more direct. They were those who believed that the occasion should be seized to establish a disciplined armed force that would be ready at any favourable moment to strike another blow for Ireland's freedom. This group, though probably not the largest section of the early recruits, were, all now know, the most earnest and persevering, and it is to their devotion and sacrifice that we are most indebted for that freedom which we here enjoy today.

De Valera himself clearly came into the first category, and, did he but know it, had little reason to thank the third, the IRB, whose earnestness and perseverence had already cost him his seat on the Gaelic League executive. But the third would use the Volunteers to draw in more and more of the first category to their own ranks, ultimately and briefly including de Valera himself. As to the second category, the analysis is sound enough, although it includes a back-handed swipe at MacNeill, for whom Father Martin's volume was in part a further count in his nationalist rehabilitation. MacNeill would form part of the Cosgrave government which prosecuted the Civil War of 1922–23 against de Valera and his anti-Treaty associates. His place in the nationalist pantheon accordingly would be heavily undermined by de Valera's propagandists during his years of power. As President, de Valera in 1963 had no choice but to acquiesce in the posthumous vindication of MacNeill in the commemoration of the Irish Volunteers, but he diminished it here with characteristic subtlety by reminding his audience that MacNeill had a wildly romantic view of Carson's Volunteers. In his anxiety to perform the Irish equivalent of preventing the Whig dogs from getting the best of it, he conceded—did he realize he was conceding?—a rather different point. He was testifying to the intransigence of Protestant Ulster, and by implication confessing the futility of so much of his own anti-partition rhetoric. But he was consistent with his real view of Protestant Ulster, which never shared the interest or the optimism of the Catholic Ulsterman MacNeill in the idea of its reconciliation with a Catholic Ireland mobilized to new nationalist fervour; from time to time he found it necessary to appear to share it, but he spoke his real mind in 1963. The plain people of Ireland agreed with him, and there was a riot in Cork when MacNeill called for cheers for Carson in salutation for his having mobilized an Irish spirit of manly self-reliance.

So there was nothing particularly inconsistent in de Valera's joining the Irish Volunteers at the moment of its inception: so did many other Home Rulers. Nor was there anything inconsistent in John Redmond and the leadership of the Irish Parliamentary Party attempting to take it over after its initial recruitment had proved so much of a success. What none of them knew was that the IRB had been directing the movement from the outset. De Valera had been thrilled by the opening meeting, quite apart from its promise of insurance of a Home Rule Ireland in which the new spirit of Gaelic enthusiasm would receive more substantial support in the matter of university appointments. He was a child of his times to the extent of rallying to the appeals to Irish military tradition. Underneath the emphasis of unity of tradition with the Ulster Protestants on which MacNeill made so much in his speech at the founding meeting in the Rotunda on 25 November 1913, there was a more obvious legacy of the diet of militaristic British literature on which Irish children were being brought up: the anxiety to show that in an actual confrontation, the Irish Catholics would wipe out the memories of shameful defeat at Newtownbutler, the Boyne, Aughrim and other purple passages in the writings of Macaulay, to say nothing of more recent misfortunes in the rebellion of 1798, 1803 and the 'cabbage-garden' *débâcle* which constituted the Irish contribution to the year of revolutions 1848. There was remarkable doublethink in the whole business, what with MacNeill's cheerful allusions to 1798 at the 25 November meeting to show the gallant Irish antecedents of Ulster Protestantism while so many of his hearers identified its memory with Catholic armed insurrection against the British connection now the focal point of Ulster Protestant intransigence.[12]

De Valera was duly enrolled into the organization, only to discover to his disgust that it was under the name of 'Emin Dilvara': however much the Volunteers might have been infiltrated by the IRB, they clearly needed more recruits from the Gaelic League. Possibly the prevailing militarism assumed a parental enthusiasm for the Emin Pasha Relief Expedition. In any case he quickly ensured that his name became conspicuous. His tall form, rendered remarkably attractive by an elegant moustache, caught attention, as did his zeal in instructing youths in the arts of 'forming fours' with his head adorned by a Sherlock Holmes deerstalker. He rose in the ranks, and exhibited coolness in command during the testing business of unloading the guns imported to Howth from Germany on 26 July 1914. Here again there was imitation of Carson, whose followers had already brought in a far larger haul of arms at Larne from the same source. De Valera's superior officer was Thomas MacDonagh.

De Valera's reticence about his private associations and influences has thrown a veil over his connection with MacDonagh. Historians have been content to assume that his continued insistence in taking all his decisions on MacDonagh's instructions until MacDonagh's execution after the 1916 Rising was the product of his devotion to protocol. But let us remember the evidence of the actor's son, Macready. De Valera throughout his life found protocol an excellent means of dictating courses of action against which no serious charge could therefore be easily sustained. But he knew perfectly well when to set it aside. His relationship with MacDonagh ultimately drove him to the acceptance of what looked like certain death. De Valera's insistence on following MacDonagh ultimately involved disobedience to their superior officer Eoin MacNeill, in the matter of starting the insurrection. He made it clear that he was ready for it to involve disobedience to their other superior officer, Patrick Pearse, in the matter of concluding the insurrection. The inference is clear. He did not follow MacDonagh because MacDonagh was his superior officer. He followed his superior officer because his superior officer was MacDonagh. After MacDonagh was dead, he followed himself.

To Thomas MacDonagh, therefore, belongs the credit of setting on foot de Valera's entire public career in Irish politics, and he merits a good, hard look. The connection is obvious enough. To geographical common ground with MacDonagh there was added the Rockwell connection. They had had experiences in common, all the more likely to bind them together because they had not overlapped, and each could contribute parts of the Rockwell story unknown to the other. De Valera had been exceptionally happy at Rockwell: he was known to allude to it as the happiest time of his life, evidently thinking in terms of location in contrast to the alien Dublin which imprisoned him for the rest of his life, when he was not in prison elsewhere. There were not only Rockwell friends in common: there were others, such as Smithwick. Beyond that, we have to assume that their startling contrast increased their regard for one another. MacDonagh was small, de Valera was tall; MacDonagh was garrulous, de Valera was reticent; MacDonagh was gregarious, de Valera was remote; MacDonagh was literary, de Valera was mathematical; MacDonagh was poetic, de Valera was prosy; MacDonagh seemed to know everyone, de Valera had difficulty in knowing anyone; MacDonagh was passing through a phase of religious scepticism, de Valera was a pattern of theological orthodoxy; MacDonagh was full of gossip about the personalities of the Volunteers, de Valera wanted to find out as much as he could about the Volunteers; MacDonagh completed his post-graduate degree, de Valera had not; MacDonagh had a university appointment, de Valera was merely a teacher in a women's training college; MacDonagh shot order and discipline to ribbons as a teacher, de Valera believed all he was taught about obedience to rules; MacDonagh had a quick staccato laugh, de Valera had a slow, saurian smile; MacDonagh ornamented sentence after sentence with an impulsive 'begad', de Valera was hardly ever known to use an expletive; MacDonagh had a Protestant, and—it was believed—an English, mother, de Valera had an Irish Catholic mother; MacDonagh came from a united family of schoolteachers, de Valera came from a divided family of labourers; MacDonagh had been loved by his mother, and never returned after her death to Cloughjordan de Valera . . .

In height, in aesthetics, in linguistic felicity, in culture, in cosmopolitanism, MacDonagh remarkably typified what de Valera could discover about his unknown father. The relationship does not seem to have fully ripened until 1915, according to the best source we have—the revealing Irish text of de Valera's authorized biography. An instructive term is employed: MacDonagh 'suited' de Valera. It is a term schoolboys used of special friendships at that date or (characteristically for de Valera) somewhat earlier. There is also a fact which is given play as a metaphor: MacDonagh enjoyed being on the stage, de Valera preferred to be in the wings. But neither of them, although they did not yet know it, had a hand in the direction of the play which they had entered. Much was concealed from MacDonagh because it was believed he could not keep his mouth shut.[13] The secret Military Council of the IRB which was planning an insurrection did not co-opt MacDonagh until the week before it was scheduled to commence. There was much that de Valera did not know. But he apparently remained satisfied to act as MacDonagh told him. He even insisted on it. MacDonagh tried to get him to join the executive committee of the Volunteers, but de Valera remained firm on that point. He was not risking the wound of another rejection, following assurance of certain success. MacDonagh would find out what was to be done, and if he told de Valera to do it, de Valera would do it. In a sense he had chosen the better part. Others swirled, conspired, rose, fell, found fruition or were broken in the preparations for the Rising. De Valera settled for subordination to the most fascinating English-language poet and critic who ever participated in an Irish insurrection. As Yeats wrote of MacDonagh in his 'Easter 1916' having first said a word on Pearse:

> This other his helper and friend
> Was coming into his force;
> He might have won fame in the end,
> So sensitive his nature seemed,
> So daring and sweet his thought.

He brought de Valera into the Rising. But what brought *him* in?

The Easter Week Rising began in the streets, not of Dublin but of Sarajevo. The connection is not only one of cause, but of kind. Professor Vladimir Dedijer concludes his magnificent *The Road to Sarajevo* by coupling the names of Gavrilo Princip and his fellow-conspirators in the cause of Slavic nationalism with those of Connolly and Pearse, and there is kinship between the origins of their conspiracies, so inept in their execution, so cataclysmic in their consequences. But the assassination of the Austrian Archduke has another relevance to MacDonagh: it unleashed throughout Europe an orgy of self-immolation on the altar of patriotism. MacDonagh's poetry of the joy of mortal combat echoes similar sentiments of Rupert Brooke and Charles Péguy; and with much less poetic expression, thousands of young men across Europe rushed for the colours and the chance of death with an exultation as fierce as theirs. In fact, the Easter Week Rising was an intensely *British* episode, quite apart from the British births of Clarke and Connolly, the British ancestral part-origin of Pearse, MacDonagh, Cathal Brugha, the brothers Boland, and others. In fighting against Britain, the Easter insurgents responded to the same mood which led so many to fight for Britain. The ideals were the same: militarism, honour, patriotism, self-sacrifice, manhood, adventure, and above all a desire to testify to spiritual yearnings defying the grey calculations of a secure and cautious life. Combat and death had become world-wide faiths. Ireland had taken her place among the nations of the earth. She had simply chosen to do so when the nations of the earth were at the height of suicidal irrationality.

That is to say, Ireland as seen in the minds of a tiny minority of her sons and daughters had chosen to do so. A much larger percentage of her sons had acted on her behalf in the more customary sense of fighting for the government of the day against its chosen enemy. The Easter insurgents reversed the usual choice of enemies and allies; otherwise, they followed suit.

Redmond threw the support of the Irish Volunteers to Asquith at the beginning of the war; a minority under MacNeill split, and that minority dwindled. De Valera saw the forty or so of his own company subordinates who had opposed Redmond at the split trickle down to six or seven. To put it at its crudest, the playing at soldiers could not compete with the real thing. Redmond was offering common sacrifice with the British to be rewarded by Home Rule in place of the earlier possibility of civil strife. De Valera might have joined up, paradoxically, had he not joined the Volunteers earlier; he now knew enough of the frailty of the promise of Home Rule to doubt its arrival as a post-bellum Long Service and Good Conduct medal. The threatened mutiny of British Officers in the Curragh before the guns had come to Larne and Howth, against the suggestion that they might have to fight kith and kin in Ulster, was a lesson from which obvious results were drawn. De Valera had little in common with the blood-sacrifice ideals of Pearse and their poetic expression by MacDonagh, however much he came to extol the former in theory and be fascinated by the latter in practice. Nor did he share the intransigent commitment to a Republic which saw the war as its great opportunity, which Tom Clarke and Seán MacDermott held. With a labourer's realistic eye he does seem to have shared some of the thinking of James Connolly, who had seen his dreams of a socialist Europe shattered when the workers joyfully took up arms against one another, and who was convinced that the war would bring galloping reaction in its wake. The Asquith government did nothing to discourage this assumption by co-opting Carson, and his principal English Tory ally, F.E. Smith, to serve as its principal Law Officers in 1915. De Valera would not have shared Connolly's Socialism, though he knew enough of its rhetoric to maintain a pull on the affections of Labour then and later: but he could see Irish Home Rule being destroyed by the war as fully as Connolly could see the obliteration of Socialism. He did resemble MacDonagh in responding to the war itself in the deepening of his involvement with the military ideal. The growing militarism induced by war meant that the barrage of British propaganda against the non-combatant deepened the resolve of the Irish Volunteer remnant to show their prowess as combatants. As matters stood, it was galling to think that the British were showing their 'manhood' while the Volunteers were still playing at soldiers.[14]

Well, if they wanted to play big boys' games, Clarke and MacDermott would oblige them. Firstly, the pressure on winning IRB recruits increased. The Gaelic League was formally politicized; the noble Douglas Hyde, whose preaching and translations had done more than any other single factor to bring back the dying Irish language to use and recourse, was displaced from its Presidency in 1915. MacNeill took his place, but MacNeill's own Volunteers were being quietly picked off and warned of the chance of much more serious and secret intentions than MacNeill must know. De Valera was invited to join the IRB. He refused. Then MacDonagh asked him. He accepted. He did not like it, but he did it. MacDonagh swore him in. But even the IRB was now becoming a dupe of its own Military Council, which was concealing its work from the Supreme Council and the straw President created by Clarke and MacDermott, Denis McCullough. Casement in Germany was intended to recruit strong support from the Kaiser's government. A Rising would take place. The IRB itself was, by its nature, hostile to notions of a *coup d'état* which defied prevailing national sentiment; but that meant nothing to Clarke, whose imprisonment had been for involvement in civilian bombing campaigns in Britain in 1883, and nothing to MacDermott, whose demonic energy in quest of a *coup* seemed if anything to have increased when he was crippled by polio. MacDermott intrigued so ably that it is still very doubtful how much was known by his dupes. Many men lose their lives in war because they believe the lies of propaganda: but seldom has there been so clear a connection between the lies and the deaths as happened in 1916. When the insurrection actually took place, Éamonn Ceannt justified it to the Volunteers under his command (who had found themselves fighting with no prior warning) by explaining that the British had decided on negotiation with the Germans following a secret session of the House of Commons, and if Ireland were only in arms it would be at the peace conference. The Rising itself was explained to Volunteer leaders during the week that preceded it, by the flourishing of a document proposing the suppression of the Volunteers and Connolly's Citizen Army (formed against the brutality of the police in the 1913 Lock-out): the 'Castle document' was forged by Plunkett. McCullough, again on the eve of rebellion, became wise to some clandestine design, and having run MacDermott down with great difficulty, was informed that the Germans would send 250 officers with a German submarine coming up the Liffey. They lied and lied to the wretched MacNeill: there would not be a Rising, then there would be a massively German-supported Rising, then when on the capture of Casement and the loss of the contemptible arms supply from Germany MacNeill countermanded the manoeuvres under which the Rising was intended to take place they lied again about obeying him. Connolly had nothing to do with the lies: he made it all too clear that he intended to have an insurrection if nobody else would as a desperate hope of stalling the forces of reaction in their tracks, but they managed to hold him back, probably by lying to him too.

Was de Valera dupe or liar in all of this? Certainly if he was among the liars his was a petty affair, nothing comparable to the, by now, pathological performances of MacDermott, or the grand design by which Clarke, having failed to lay London in ruins, would find an alternative in Dublin. In fairness to Clarke and MacDermott, they stand within their own terrifying logic, in classical conspiratorial fashion. To Pearse, all was secondary to the holy cause of the sacrifice which would end the torture that his life had become. But the others had at least the excuse that they well knew from the analyses of Casement and others how vast was the lying on the British propaganda side, especially with reference to supposed atrocities in Belgium, something of particularly pointed interest to Casement because of his previous disclosures of actual atrocities by the Belgian King in the Congo. The excuse does not seem to have been made: MacNeill would hardly have been reconciled to his own officers Pearse and MacDonagh being proved liars by the reminder that Asquith was another. Indeed the whole basis of Irish nationalism was that its purity set it above British materialism and venality.

We cannot ignore the fact that de Valera's entire political career had begun by a baptism, not only of fire, but of ethics of this kind. Richard Mulcahy (afterwards the General leading the suppression of de Valera's anti-Treaty friends in the Civil War and later still leader of the Opposition to the de Valera Government in the 1940s) never forgot how de Valera met him shortly after his election to Dáil Éireann in 1919 with the advice: 'You are a young man going in for politics. I will give you two pieces of advice—study economics and read the *Prince*.' The charge of discipleship to Machiavelli was perpetually thrown at de Valera by his enemies throughout his political life. Yet the remark has an entirely different connotation: it could well be the bitter statement of a man who saw himself surrounded by disciples of Machiavelli, and felt forced to read him in order to understand the ethics with which he would have to deal in political life as put forward by friends or foes. De Valera as the heir to the Easter Rising could never afford to tell what he knew of the Machiavellianism of Seán MacDermott, still less to denounce it. He showed his real feelings only by withdrawing from the IRB, oath or no oath, after his release from imprisonment in 1917, by trying to draw his close associates out of it, and later by avenging himself on Clarke and MacDermott in fostering the cult of Pearse at their expense. It was of course Pearse the rhetorician and writer he built up, not Pearse the liar and tool of MacDermott. Above all he came to abhor the manipulation, the secrecy and the hidden loyalties concealed from followers. This is not to say that some of MacDermott's Machiavellianism did not rub off on de Valera: indeed his use of the cult of the martyrs, and his selectivity about it, had its Machiavellian character.

In 1916 what de Valera knew of the deceptions must in fact have been very small. For MacDonagh knew little of them. The open-hearted, open-tongued poet seems largely to have been an easy prey to the smiling, lying conspirator. Ruth Dudley Edwards suggests that MacDonagh probably believed in the Castle document when he gave it publicity, even though he was now a brand new co-option to the Military Council, and her argument is impressive, for after MacDonagh took part in the deception of MacNeill on Easter Sunday as to the decision to hold the insurrection in defiance of his countermand, he wrote a letter recording his deception and unhappiness that it should be necessary. He corrected his use of the word 'obligation' and substituted 'intention' with respect to acting 'with my own Council and the position of that Council': he was not going to wriggle off the hook of responsibility. The letter was first read a year later in the presence of de Valera, who may not have known until then that MacDonagh had privately deceived MacNeill as well as publicly accepting the countermand for Easter Sunday but then acting on Easter Monday. 'I have guarded secrets which I am bound to keep', wrote MacDonagh, 'I have, I think, acted honourably and fairly by all my associates'. Only de Valera could judge that, as far as it related to himself—and it was clearly he above all whom MacDonagh had in mind here, even more than his colleagues on the Military Council. De Valera in 1917 probably took comfort that the letter ended with a prayer 'to God for the gifts of counsel and fortitude, and for His blessing on the cause of my country': MacDonagh had in his crisis returned to the faith of his fathers, now and not simply at the hour of his death. Perhaps de Valera knew more of that return, and had even assisted in it, than we can ever know. But he was finished with secrecy, if he could help it—he hoped.

MacNeill can have had little cause to complain of de Valera's conduct as regards the deception: de Valera openly refused to accept the countermand without orders from MacDonagh when MacNeill directed him so to do. If anything, de Valera's attitude should have warned MacNeill that something more of the supposedly aborted insurrection was likely to be heard. But MacNeill would not have known that de Valera actually opposed the insurrection, and only agreed to take part when MacDonagh specifically asked him to. Clearly, de Valera would not have disheartened his men, when the Rising began, by telling them how hopeless the whole thing was, what with Casement's capture and Germany's obvious indifference to anything save luring Britain into discreditable repression. It is possible that he may have informed them of the belief that the British would not destroy capitalist property: but in retrospect while recording that the belief was prevalent he told T.P. O'Neill he himself had not held it. Nor do his actions in the Rising indicate that he did. He said that the view was propounded by Connolly, and his recollection has been taken seriously by historians: but wherever he got it, he was surely mistaken in that. P.S. O'Hegarty in his *History of Ireland Under the Union* recalled hearing the thesis from MacDermott, and it has every hallmark of probability that this was its origin. No doubt MacDermott might have alleged it came from Connolly, when talking to people impressed by Connolly. But in fact Connolly was quite certain that the British would bombard undefended towns, and said as much in the *Worker,* in his 'Can Warfare be Civilized?' on 30 January 1915. He noted elsewhere that private property destroyed in war would be awarded compensation. It was believed by MacDonagh, who happily burbled about it to Desmond FitzGerald, but MacDonagh's intelligence had nothing to do with the realities of world politics and economics. It suited de Valera to believe he heard it from Connolly, probably imposing what he had heard from MacDonagh on some typical piece of heavy Marxist sarcasm from Connolly; his recollection, like many men's, became in part at least the unconscious servant of his desires. He could not say MacDermott was a liar; he did not want to say MacDonagh was a fool. But it suited him to say Connolly was brave but misguided. His subordinate in Boland's Mills, George A. Lyons, invented numerous conversations along these lines in his *Some Recollections of Griffith and his Times* with Griffith as the quizzical Socrates and Connolly as the bovine Thrasymachus. De Valera did not contradict such legends: it suited him to have the Socialist leader praised for his spirit but to have Labour reassured that its destiny would be better served in wiser hands. In any case de Valera's memories of the Rising were inevitably confused by its complications. He had known of talk of an insurrection long before he was drawn into one. He later wished his leaders had been more open, therefore he made them so. And he wanted to appear less innocent himself. In the end his reason for going into the rising was Thomas MacDonagh, but he could not in retrospect show himself so immature.[15]

And he did enter it an innocent. There is little sign about him of Connolly's grim mutter to his non-combatant colleague William O'Brien 'we are going out to be slaughtered' (no confidence in Britain's withholding bombardment from Dublin about that!). What de Valera did show when he occupied Boland's Mills while Pearse at the General Post Office was reading the Proclamation of the Republic on behalf of the Provisional Government (true to the Carsonite model), was a fine defensive military leadership. He had been given an enormous area to control. Connolly, Commanding General at Headquarters in the General Post Office, summed it up on Friday 28 April, the fifth day of the Rising, almost certainly with a characteristic flicker of grim humour, for he too was a short man and de Valera's height was notorious:

> Commandant de Valera stretches in a position from the Gas Works in Westland Row, holding Boland's Bakery, Boland's Mills, Dublin South-Eastern Railway Works and dominating Merrion Square.

By that time Connolly himself was in great pain from a wounded leg, and the Post Office itself was doomed. But de Valera had had a very successful week. Darrell Figgis in his *Recollections of the Irish War* singles him out as one of the two commanders in specific Dublin sites who had brought imagination to his work, the other being Clarke's brother-in-law Edward Daly at the Four Courts. He began with his characteristic reactionary romanticism, having a tram taken over by pikemen. In a sense, he closed it the same way, for after surrender he was overheard supposedly saying 'if only the people had come out with knives and forks'. In fact, urban Dublin misheard the rural reference: de Valera insisted—and surely he is to be believed on this—that what he actually said was 'come out with hay forks'. But his real genius showed itself in the stratagem by which having diagnosed that a building adjoining his Boland's headquarters would make an ideal point of attack for the enemy, he had an Irish green flag run up on it and saw it flattened by the British bombardment and hence incapable of occupation. Perhaps this was also a legacy of the country, where there would be more schoolboy knowledge of the tactics of open space.

On the other hand, his logic caused him problems. His insistence that his troops detailed to seize Westland Row Station should take any uniformed soldiers as prisoners, meant that he cluttered himself up with a nice cadet called G.F. Mackay who had to be guarded carefully for the rest of the week. The historian must be nevertheless grateful to him, for Cadet Mackay on his release after the Rising gave an interview testifying to the firm command maintained by 'Commandant Devileur'. There was no drink, there was a good spirit and 'Devileur' seemed tireless. He had had time to nerve himself for the ordeal since he had known of the impending insurrection since the previous Wednesday, had taken his leave of his wife and four children and had been fortified by making his Confession to a priest in University Church. Most of the 120-odd who had reported to his command should have deduced from the countermand of Easter Sunday manoeuvres and the call to parade on Easter Monday that something critical was to the fore, and with the prevailing loose talk about an insurrection they might have deduced what: the fact that de Valera was supposed to be leading 500 indicated the conclusion to which many Volunteers had come. MacDonagh, characteristically, had even told his own company on the preceding Wednesday that they would turn out on the Sunday and that some of them might not come back. MacDonagh's honesty, no less than MacNeill's countermand, was believed to have cost the insurgents dear, but as perhaps the greatest historian of the Rising, the late Maureen Wall, pointed out, this meant that those who wanted to participate could do so then or later and that the rest should have realized something very serious was on foot. But de Valera had to allow for involuntary insurgents who were nevertheless surprised by the fighting but did not want to abandon their comrades. So he needed full vigilance to counteract the effects of his men having been given so little, if any, advance warning. At one point he discovered that sentinels had withdrawn from their posts to take part in the saying of the Rosary, clearly to raise morale and provide for spiritual insurance against sudden death; and he had to persuade them to return. At least they knew that he was in full spiritual accord with them. Then there was the problem of Mackay: the British forces, not reinforced with the artillery of the *Helga* on the Liffey until Wednesday, believed the insurgent forces occupying the various Dublin buildings were far larger than was in fact the case. It was not realized that MacNeill had been wholly genuine in countermanding the Easter Sunday manoeuvres and that his action had given the majority of the Volunteers an opportunity to stay out of the fighting which they had accepted. So if Mackay escaped, the sequel could be an immediate assault, and his evidence as to the small number under 'Devileur' would be applied to the rest of the Rising. Ceannt in the South Dublin Union greatly benefited from the British assumptions of much larger forces than he had. Hence Mackay found his life threatened, although he was treated with dignity.[16]

Unlike MacDonagh, who with the Second Battalion was largely 'dug into' Jacob's Biscuit Factory (in which he was fairly impregnable but unable to take much offensive action), de Valera indeed 'stretched' far beyond Boland's. In particular, a small detachment was placed at Mount Street Bridge where by bluff and surprise they played havoc with the incoming soldiery along the Southern approaches. What happened was far uglier than de Valera probably knew, for the British higher command had been even more reticent than Ceannt about what lay ahead of the troops so that recruits marching north from their landing at Kingstown (Dún Laoghaire) in what they understood to be a part of their own country, suddenly found themselves being shot to pieces. The regimental history insists that the officer commanding was not surprised by the attack; it is clear that his men were. If anything, many of them had had less training, and certainly for a far shorter period, than the Volunteers themselves. Ultimately the British won that battle, and closed in on Boland's Mills. Morale began to go to pieces and nerves to snap: one man is reported to have shot a comrade and been killed when he attacked a sentry, another to have fired madly around him with a small revolver before he was forcibly disarmed. De Valera got a message to MacDonagh saying he was running low on bullets and expecting an attack, but while MacDonagh tried to send a small party to his aid—on bicycles—they could not get through. De Valera looked at the prospect of linking up with the insurgents in St Stephen's Green, but this was also impossible. He contemplated a retreat from the bakery, and on Friday a temporary withdrawal took place to be greeted by the sight of a sea of flame over the city; but for all of de Valera's energy in commanding the southern approaches it was clear that the only chance that now remained to them was to stay 'dug in' in their turn. It seems fairly clear that he expected to be killed with his men in a final assault. He was even about to shave on Sunday 30 April in anticipation of it—the elegant moustache had now sprouted to a ferocious length, which together with his name no doubt accounted for the widespread Dublin impression (remembering reports of Pancho Villa and Zapata in 1915) that the insurgents in Boland's were commanded by a Mexican. But his toilet was interrupted by the arrival of an envoy from General Lowe with a message signed by Pearse telling him to surrender. He refused: the message was not signed by MacDonagh.

Pearse certainly intended that everyone would surrender at his word. It is not clear that Connolly did: he accepted unconditional surrender for 'the men under my own command' and, wounded, wrote in the word 'only' after 'men' which effectively limited his instructions to St Stephen's Green and the city centre. If others could and would keep on fighting Connolly would seem to have been prepared to let them. Whether de Valera saw a hint in that additional 'only' or not is beside the point; MacDonagh might see one, and take it, but it was for MacDonagh to tell de Valera whether or not to remain on the burning deck. While Pearse had surrendered on

Saturday at 3.00pm, fourteen hours later MacDonagh, quite ignorant of the fact, was exultantly awaiting his doom. 'Small actions seem to be developing against my right', he reported in a despatch to St Stephen's Green. 'Thank God, as we are tired of sniping.' But what duly arrived several hours later still was the instruction from Pearse. MacDonagh in his turn was bitterly disappointed and was tempted to go on; he saw Lowe at noon, then he saw Ceannt who left the decision to himself. It would have been very difficult for him to consult with de Valera: Pearse's emissary, Elizabeth O'Farrell, although proceeding with the full co-operation of the British, had found it very hard to approach de Valera and another long trail to reach MacDonagh. But in fact by the time MacDonagh surrendered to Lowe, at 3.00pm, de Valera was in British hands. There had been a conference of officers; and it evidently went against him.[17]

With the aid of Mackay he made contact with the authorities and surrendered himself and his men, giving Mackay his revolver in a gesture at once touching and sinister, with the request that he transmit it at some time to his son Vivion. So by 2.00pm he was in Ballsbridge under guard in the Weights and Measures section in the Town Hall, while his 117 Volunteers were being confined to horse-boxes in the Horse Show grounds. Whether MacDonagh possessed the knowledge that his faithful de Valera had been unable to hold support for him in Boland's and this was a further cause of his tears of rage and mortification as he agreed to surrender, we do not know. No more do we know whether he realized with what classically filial devotion, regardless of the mere two years between them, his friend had so consistently placed his will in MacDonagh's hands up to now. Almost certainly they never saw each other again. It was not until 2 May that de Valera was taken to Richmond Barracks; MacDonagh was court-martialled there that morning and sent to Kilmainham where he was shot the next day. So were Pearse and Clarke. They were the first of fifteen. A British officer was later quoted as having said, 'They all died well, but MacDonagh died like a prince'.[18]

De Valera was fairly certain that he would be shot too. As the executions mounted up under martial law, names of persons who had played a far less conspicuous part than himself appeared on the lists: Pearse's brother Willie and Michael O'Hanrahan among the dead on 4 May, Con Colbert on 8 May. His own court-martial took place on the day Colbert (and Ceannt and Mallin of the St Stephen's Green command and the 25-year-old Seán Heuston) had been shot. De Valera had taken leave of his fellow-prisoners in Richmond Barracks, many of them begging souvenirs of him down to his buttons. At his hearing, the United States Consul appeared in recognition of Sinéad's claim to him that her husband was an American citizen, and later informed the State Department that this ensured de Valera's commutation of sentence of death to imprisonment for life. De Valera never admitted this possibility, citing the simultaneous pardon of his fellow-Commandant Thomas Ashe, but Ashe had been responsible for far less slaughter in the affray at Ashbourne than de Valera's campaign in the city. Pressure was mounting in horror at the executions from many who had fiercely denounced the insurgents. De Valera had not won the attention of Dublin Castle spies before the Rising: he was, so to say, an unmarked man. Redmond is said to have interceded for him. But he lay at the mercy of General Sir John Maxwell, who had superseded the civilian government in Dublin Castle during the Rising. Maxwell, coincidentally, was more alive to the delicacies of placating American opinion, in the hope of American entry into the war, than any other British general, perhaps than any person in the British government. Maxwell's daughter (and sole offspring) Philae had fallen in love with a young American named C.N. Carver, who after a year at Cambridge followed, when war had broken out, by another in the US embassy in London, was now an aide to President Wilson's trusted personal emissary Colonel House. (She married him.) As a soldier, Maxwell knew how vital respect for the representations of American officialdom would be to ensure that so indispensable a potential ally was not needlessly alienated. So he did not confirm the death sentence, as he would naturally have done in conformity with the procedure which had taken the lives of that morning's four victims. De Valera was probably right in seeing a connection between Ashe's pardon and his own, but it was the converse which applied. Once de Valera had been made an exception to the principle of execution for the leaders, Ashe could hardly be given the extreme penalty. It would be otherwise with the still surviving Connolly and MacDermott, who as the remaining two signatories of the Proclamation of the Republic were as much beyond pardon as the unrepentant signatories of the death-warrant of Charles I. They died on 12 May.[19]

De Valera owed much more than his life to Maxwell. By his severity, the British General had caused revulsion in Irish feeling so violent that the most conspicuous leader he had pardoned was automatically set on the path to political triumph in the East Clare election one year later. But to get there de Valera had to make at least some decisions himself. No longer could the vital questions be determined by the instructions of a surrogate father. But the months ahead were long, long months, and for all of the companionship of his fellow-prisoners he must have yearned for the sound of that staccato laugh, and the excited, electric 'begad!'

And what but a fool was I, crying defiance to Death,
Who shall lead my soul from this calm to mingle with God's very breath!
Who shall lead me thither perhaps while you are waiting here still,
Sighing for thought of me when the winds are out on the hill.

3

Arma Virumque Cano

'. . .
sum pius Aeneas, raptos qui ex hoste penatis
classe veho mecum, fama super aethera notus.
Italiam quaero patriam et genus ab Iove summo.
. . .'
                              ille ubi matrem
agnovit tali fugientem est voce secutus:
'quid natum totiens, crudelis tu quoque falsis
ludis imaginibus? cur dextrae iungere dextram
non datur ac veras audire et reddere voces?'

           —P. Vergilii Maronis, *Aeneidos* I. 378–80, 405–09.

When the Dawn is Come. A Tragedy in Three Acts

           —Title of play by Thomas MacDonagh (1908)

MacNeill had given himself up, was tried and sentenced, and arrived some weeks after the others. De Valera heard his voice when being inducted. The next day the prisoners were standing in their wing before going to exercise. The Dartmoor wings are so laid out that one man breaking ranks is seen instantly by all the rest. MacNeill appeared. De Valera swung out of line, gave the parade command 'Eyes left'. They did it, automatically. Prison cultivates discipline. De Valera was ordered back to his cell. He was threatened by the authorities, but not punished. It gave him three victories. He was a leader: his Irish fellow-prisoners recognized it. The authorities recognized it, and hence he would be watched, but not provoked. Provocation of prisoners' leader meant risking riot. The Governor had said his command was mutiny. The Governor was afraid of mutiny. And MacNeill recognized it. The men who had defied his countermand were made to honour him. It was a peace gesture. The dissidents would honour MacNeill. So if ever they got out MacNeill should not repudiate them. If there was any future it had to be in nationalist unity. MacNeill would command respect. Opponents of the Rising would find it unfair that the man who tried to stop it had been punished. MacNeill's friends would be their friends.

It is not easy to retain leadership in prison. Fortunately the authorities could be a help. De Valera was detected giving food to another prisoner. He was placed on a diet of bread and water for three days. Here was a chance to consolidate his leadership by a personal sacrifice. This time he would involve nobody but himself. He would go on hunger strike. It was an honoured weapon. Sheehy-Skeffington had done it. The British soldiers had killed Sheehy-Skeffington during the Rising, although as a pacifist he had opposed it. Opponents of the Rising would not like that.

Sheehy-Skeffington: Father Eugene had been his wife's uncle. It would not be easy to go on hunger strike. And thirst strike. That would make it much nastier, but much quicker. He kept it up for three days. He was sent to the infirmary and was then transferred to Maidstone. He was chained to Desmond FitzGerald, and to Dr Richard Hayes, who was interested in Irish links with France. FitzGerald had been in the General Post Office during the Rising. He could have told de Valera that Pearse had talked of a German Prince ruling Ireland if they were successful. So much for a Republic. Certainly de Valera showed no further interest in wartime aid from Germany. He would be very annoyed when the British later stated he did.

He was only briefly at Maidstone, and then was sent to Lewes, together with many other Irish prisoners. Here, de Valera instructed the Governor in geology and was given permission to study mathematics. He protested against the prison food, and called a work strike when a prisoner was put on bread and water. He warned the others against hunger strikes. He got more news of Ireland and sent letters out secretly. He wrote on the wall of his cell: $i^2 = j^2 = k^2 = ijk = -1$ (Rowan Hamilton's formula). He brooded about it. He would have enjoyed explaining it to warders, who would have found it a contrast to customary convict murals. He heard of the birth of a new son, Ruairi, in November, named in memory of Casement.

But what was happening in Ireland? He wrote a long letter to Simon Donnelly, his aide in Boland's Mills. Donnelly he knew and trusted: they had been through fire together. In politics, nobody else was left. His wife was not political. He did not wish her to be. She was no longer even living in Dublin, having moved to the privacy of Greystones, co. Wicklow. The children would be less likely to endure taunts about their father being a convict. He knew taunts to children about their parents. His letter to Donnelly was smuggled out in sacred scapulars worn by Gerald Crofts, the singer, released because of ill-health. As ever, he saw religious observance as his natural ally. He chose a date sacred in religion and now in patriotism: Easter Sunday, the appointed day for the Rising before MacNeill countermanded. He had not favoured the Rising. He was a reluctant Republican. He had probably believed in the 'Castle document' and hence saw the Rising as a defensive measure to protect the Volunteers. But now he was custodian of the Rising and of the Republic it had proclaimed:

> We regard ourselves as at present, in a very special way, identified with the cause, the ideals and aspirations for which our comrades died last Easter. We feel that any important action of ours will, too, have a reflex effect on last Easter's sacrifice and on any advantages which have been secured by that

sacrifice. To do anything which would be liable to be misinterpreted and misrepresented—to create a wrong impression as to the ideals, principles and opinions which prompted last Easter's action would, it seems to us, be a national calamity.

He had not been an enthusiast for blood-sacrifice: now he had to make the most of its possible gains. He had a following. But what was he to do with either his inheritance or his followers?

He had believed in the Irish Volunteers, as a means for maintaining pressure for Irish nationalist aspirations:

The armed force started in 1913 must not be allowed to disappear. The Irish Volunteers, or whatever else you like to call them, must be kept as a permanent force at the country's back. That it seems to us is our mission as a body and we must allow nothing to make us forget it.

Events were moving without him. Just before Christmas, had died the septuagenarian James J. O'Kelly, MP, former crack American journalist, former Clan-na-Gael (neo-Fenian) activist, and from 1880 constitutionalist politician who was Parnell's closest friend. The by-election in Roscommon North had been contested by George Noble Plunkett, largely on his being the father of one executed and two imprisoned Easter insurgents. In early February, Count Plunkett had defeated two opponents with a vote of 3,022 as against 1,708 for the Redmondite. It was a 'sympathy' vote of the kind de Valera would use *ad nauseam* to elect relatives of Republican martyrs and later of Fianna Fáil deputies dying in office. But it alarmed him now. Plunkett was assisted by Griffith of Sinn Féin, but had refused to give a pre-election pledge that he would not take his seat at Westminster, as Griffith's policy decreed. His vote was probably much higher because he gave no such pledge, nor was he formally a Sinn Féin candidate. But on election he did refuse to go to Westminster. In Britain, and even Ireland, the Easter Rising had been widely, if wholly inaccurately, described as a 'Sinn Féin Rebellion', and de Valera resented any question of Sinn Féin cashing in. Of Plunkett's policy, de Valera asked Donnelly:

How far is it a reversion to the old Sinn Féin *political* movement? With his movement, or that part of it which aims at getting representative men to draw up a statement on Ireland's case for presentation at the Peace Conference, we are heartily in accord, and it seems to us that if his policy were limited to this one (and new) issue it would be endorsed by the majority of the Irish people.

This had been at least one pretext for the Rising.

Among the many prisoners in Lewes were numerous IRB men, whose faith was far more personal than that of MacDonagh's reluctant convert. Although many physical force men like O'Kelly had entered Parliament in Parnell's day, the IRB had never sanctioned such heresy. Even to stand in an election for the Westminster Parliament was believed by the purists to look like an occasion of sin. De Valera recorded their misgiving, but for all of his lack of political experience his own misgiving lay in the political sphere of the dangers of failure. Another by-election was imminent and Joseph McGuinness, who had taken part in the capture of the Four Courts at Easter and was now in Lewes with him, was being asked to stand. McGuinness was IRB and was anxious to refuse. De Valera found other reasons for Donnelly:

> It is a question whether it is good tactics (or strategy if you will) to provoke a contest in which *defeat* may well mean *ruin*.

He remembered that the last Sinn Féin candidacy he had known, in 1908, had been a disastrous defeat of a sitting candidate who had resigned when leaving Redmond for Sinn Féin. It was Sinn Féin who would nominate McGuinness.

> As soldiers we should abstain *officially* from taking sides in these contests and no candidates should in future be *officially* recognized as standing in our interests or as representing our ideals. We can individually help all those who are striving for Ireland's freedom by other means—there will never be any lack of these—but we should *as a body* keep to our own special sphere.

As for the delegates to the Peace Conference when the war should end they should demand absolute independence and if 'admitted . . . should be given no powers of agreeing to anything less'.

De Valera was the official leader in Lewes. But the quiet Thomas Ashe, of Ashbourne fame, was also there, and he was in touch with a much more formidable individual than Simon Donnelly: the youthful Michael Collins, a minor insurgent in the Rising, who after internment was quickly building up a new life for the IRB in which popular appeal by parliamentary elections had a major part to play. For the moment Collins did not prevail on McGuinness although he persuaded Ashe. But it mattered not a straw. McGuinness was nominated in his native Longford (which had supplied the sole reason for his sudden significance). Ominously, on the eve of the election Archbishop William Walsh of Dublin observed publicly that the politicians were committed to the partition of Ireland. It just tipped the scale in favour of the anti-politician, who squeaked home: otherwise, the voters would probably have rejected the abstentionist policy of Griffith. Longford was close enough to Ulster to be seriously concerned about its exclusion, or part-exclusion, from a Home Rule Ireland. But it was not combustible nationalist territory like Roscommon—or East Clare—with a history of returning luxuriantly vehement nationalists in the Redmondite ranks. The sympathy slogan for McGuinness—'put him in to get him out'—was not as good an emotive appeal as the ghost of Joseph Mary Plunkett, the slain poet. Lewes accepted the *fait accompli.*

Was de Valera at this point a militarist rather than a democrat? It seems like it. At least there is a readiness to stress the sacred character of the military body as superior to the profanity of politics. But it is doubtful if he envisaged anything more than a return of the Volunteers to their old status of an earnest of Ireland's nationalist intentions, with an essentially defensive role. He was a custodian of the Easter shrine. Others might contemplate more aggressive action. As leader, he had to be aware of their views, and there is an implication—not absolute—that he is subject to majority opinion of those views. The prisoners, as survivors of the Rising, are in part also custodians of the shrine. Their title—and this proved an ominous precedent—was clearly superior to that of the people at large as expressed in the tainted sphere of a politics in theory suspect as being British, in practice polluted by the internecine constitutionalist warfare since the Parnell split. The true destiny of Ireland was to be shaped by the Volunteers, as the heirs of the Easter Rising.

But he must have seen the limitations on his leadership when his draft of a letter of rejection of the offer of nomination to be signed by McGuinness found itself in competition with other drafts from Ashe and another major IRB figure, Diarmuid Lynch, in whose interest US Consul Adams had also intervened at court-martial. De Valera's involvement with the IRB might have perished with the rattle of gunfire which took the life of MacDonagh. That of others had not. He could ponder on MacDonagh's advice that the real policy of the Volunteers would be dictated by the IRB. That he did not wish to continue. He had every motive to mend political fences with Eoin MacNeill.

In any case the election of Joe McGuinness was a reminder to Ashe and Lynch as well as de Valera that the new Ireland evolving during their imprisonment was not going to be shackled by the thoughts of custodians of Volunteer innocence or IRB fastidiousness. (It was also a reminder to Joe McGuinness, who duly followed Collins thereafter, up to and including the acceptance of the Treaty.) It was decided by the activists outside that a work strike be called to demand status as political, indeed military, prisoners. This began on 28 May, a massive indignation meeting followed in Dublin on 10 June, and after the unsuccessful expedient of transferring de Valera and others back to Maidstone, and others still to Parkhurst, the government capitulated and their release was announced on 15 June. The gesture was a generous one, given the severity of the crimes for which sentence had been passed: but the government, now under Lloyd George, had robbed themselves of its benefits by seeming to have surrendered to firm action instead of pre-empting their opponents' indignation campaign by showing the clemency in response to McGuinness's election. Meanwhile Collins, through Ashe, had been making efforts to convince the prisoners that any use of Arthur Griffith's organization would not result in the perpetuation of its ancient enthusiasm for the dual monarchy.

De Valera had been acknowledged—on one level—as leader of a tiny nationalist group. But Lewes also gave him his very last days as a private person until his resignation from the Presidency in 1973 at the age of 91: all future imprisonments he suffered, and in all he spent about three years of his life in jail, were those of a mass leader to whose lightest utterance thousands responded in hatred or love. At Lewes any attention he won in the world outside would be as a name of which virtually nothing was known, and even the name and its origins were known but imperfectly. He was best known to the minor insurgents of the Rising interned by the British and released the preceding December, but they knew little enough. Hence it is easy to see the letter to Simon Donnelly as the product of isolation in much including its choice of recipient, but while thereafter he was quickly whirled away from its austerity (and its recipient) it laid down certain lines of thought which dictated his subsequent political style.

The Volunteers in prison are best seen as a priesthood, in his formulation. Hence his very rigid circumspection as to their political involvement. They have received the final rites of ordination by the great Sacrifice of Easter Week, with certain conspicuous exceptions like Eoin MacNeill. On the other hand there is a status for figures like MacNeill who, like those Irish Catholics declining the final step to actual ordination in the Roman Catholic priesthood, still might have a valuable part to play as some sort of learned Brother in minor orders. The vision of this priesthood as political virgins quickly disappeared—after all, the actual Roman Catholic priests were to make it very clear that, apart from candidacy for office, they were entering more actively into politics than at any time since the fall of Parnell. Even before Walsh's contribution to the McGuinness election, Father Michael O'Flanagan had been a vociferous speaker for Count Plunkett, and the most ferocious public denunciation of Maxwell had been from Bishop Edward Thomas O'Dwyer who had among other things consistently opposed Parnell, attempted to silence Father Eugene Sheehy, and given the Sacrament of Confirmation to Edward de Valera. But the idea of his followers as a priesthood still remained, and there is no reason to believe de Valera ever lost it. It is this which accounts for so much that is peculiar in de Valera's politics. He was not a particularly bitter man: in a slightly cranky, mathematical way, his sense of humour was too strong for bitterness. But he saw all defectors from his ranks as something worse than traitors: they were the accursed of all accursed, priests who had defected from their sacred calling, the false shepherds against whom Christ had warned, who fled from their charge on the approach of wolves, who became like ravening wolves themselves despite retaining a shepherd-like appearance. De Valera in prison had from the first had the use of the Bible, and of the Missal containing the service for the Sacrifice of Mass, above all the hearing of the Gospel. Hence he never felt quite the same animus against the old IRA when in power that he did against his official Opposition, the pro-Treaty Fine Gael. The old IRA would not be defectors, but extreme conservatives, who had held by the Old Law and the old rites when theological modernization required readjustment. They were wrong, but they were not of the same order of apostasy.

It might be argued that in a highly Catholic country this would be a prevalent attitude. But, however unsophisticated, most Irish politicians of the new order had obtained some form of political apprenticeship at home, even when its main effect was to inspire its own rejection. De Valera, far more than most, more even than persons who had actually entered the minor orders of Catholic priesthood only later to refuse or be denied final ordination, was a child of the Roman Catholic Church and thought in its sacred vocabulary. It must be stressed that for all of his readiness to identify the priesthood of his immediate followers with the ideal of a Republic from time to time, it was not basic to it. The Republic became a useful means of consolidating his support around an object of special devotion; but there is a great, if frequently silent, distinction between Catholic objects of special devotion and articles of faith. An object of special devotion might be pre-eminent at one time, and might receive less precedence at another; it was never explicitly repudiated, but it might be diminished in emphasis for fear of spiritual imbalance or profanation.[1]

Now de Valera could be a private person no more, for on 7 June Major Willie Redmond, MP for East Clare, had been killed fighting for the Allies at Messines. Moves began to make this a real test of strength of the new nationalism, officially campaigning under the banner of Sinn Féin, but actually including many elements in the Gaelic Athletic Association (whose local branch first mooted an anti-Redmondite candidate), the IRB, the Irish Volunteers and the Roman Catholic Church. (In a word, 'Irish-Ireland'.) The by-election was set for 10 July. It was a fortunate juxtaposition for the new nationalists, for its results would obliterate the outcome in another to be held on 6 July in South County Dublin, a seat often held by the Unionists until the second 1910 election and one in which Sinn Féin and its allies did not dare intervene for fear of splitting the nationalist vote. In the event, the South Dublin Unionists did not give their old enemies the benefit of being nationalist standard-bearers, and the uncontested Redmondite victory was forgotten. But the opportunity of popular test of the anti-Redmondite nationalist strength had to be taken in East Clare, and as de Valera had warned Donnelly any failure in such an event would be disastrous, especially in the 'banner county' of Clare where mass mobilization had elected Ireland's first Catholic to Westminster in 1828 in defiance of the ban against his religion. While Daniel O'Connell had been a great opponent of violence, he had also been the much-abused key figure of extreme Irish nationalist politics in his day. Whatever de Valera's misgivings, the new nationalists had to draw on the heirs of the Easter Rising for their standard-bearer, and they did not dare try their luck again with an obscure local man, after the close shave in Longford. It had to be a major figure, preferably with associations near the locality. De Valera's prison leadership had been growing increasingly nominal for many; but his hard personal core of support and the simple fact of leadership would be decisive here, as later.

On his release he at once showed his natural instincts for politics by two outstanding decisions: he made a strategic return visit to Bruree, about 15 miles south of the constituency, and he enlisted Eoin MacNeill as speechwriter and chief supporting speaker. Neither was as simple as it seemed. MacNeill was certainly vital behind the scenes, in keeping de Valera's rhetoric within bounds the majority of clerics would have found acceptable. The opposition tried to brand de Valera as intending to 'lead the young men into an abortive rebellion'. De Valera replied that the Easter Rising had saved 'the national soul of Ireland':

> Another Easter week would be a superfluity. He and his friends had been called wild red revolutionary Jacobites, because they said that they would not altogether eliminate physical force from their programme. Why should they eliminate it? If they did it would mean that John Bull could kick as much as he liked.

This was a firm return to the concept of the Irish Volunteers as defensive, and as moral reinforcement for nationalism.

MacNeill, above all, was needed to reassure dissident nationalists ready to vote against the Irish Parliamentary Party but unsure of de Valera's identification with full-tilt insurgent Republicanism. No doubt many clerics were in this category, but they were the smaller part of the group he was intended to corral. His presence and his advice were therefore essential: and his bitter experience in 1916 would be there to help ensure de Valera did not become the prisoner of the IRB, which de Valera himself was as anxious to avoid as MacNeill. MacNeill's piety was also timely: he stopped dead in a major speech so that the crowd could say the Angelus at 6.00pm, on which event one parish priest wrote a poem, another set it to music and the Clare *Champion* published the result.

Clare had been living in a condition of one-party politics for nearly twenty years, and had been voting Home Rule since 1880. The local MPs had been 'carpetbag', with Willie Redmond resident in Wicklow and Colonel Arthur Lynch of West Clare in London and Paris. Clearly de Valera would be 'carpetbag' too, but he would speak with a far more local voice and identification from childhood with local problems. It was the replacement of 'gentlemen' by 'one of ourselves'. The name and birthplace might be a problem, but Lynch had been born in Australia and Redmond at the other end of the country in Wexford. But in an eerie way, de Valera was not running wholly against the Irish Parliamentary Party in Clare either. The fight was one of age against youth: and the hold of the Irish Parliamentary Party over its followers depended on the long memory of affection for dedicated but inarticulate young men, more courageous than judicious, no strangers to the hostility of the police and the inside of jails. De Valera was a bad and painful speaker as yet: old men knew that Parnell had begun that way too. His Nationalist party opponent was by profession a trained and facile speaker: Clare was revolting against trained and facile speakers. Colonel Lynch had supported the Boers in South Africa and had been tried and sentenced for high treason, the prosecutor being the then Tory Solicitor-General, Carson. Lynch had supported the British war effort in the present war but after the Rising compared the insurgents in their integrity to Wolfe Tone and Emmet. But the strangest ally of all on de Valera's side was the ghost of Major Willie Redmond, whose support for Parnell had been expressed from the first in fiery nationalist speeches as popular with his constituents as they had been entertaining to his leader.

Dr David Fitzpatrick, masterly student of Clare politics in the period, is surely correct in arguing that de Valera began in East Clare his 'metamorphosis of a small, clandestine, radical élitist movement' into 'a vast, open, oddly respectable populist movement'. He began it by metamorphosing himself. He took to politics. He used his innocence to great effect. He was accepted as the simple soldier, the unworldly patriot, the prisoner of conscience. He probably did much to quieten fears of his possible involvement with European revolution (after all, 1917 was a year in which things happened elsewhere as well as in Ireland) by having apparent difficulty in distinguishing between Jacobites and Jacobins. He also gave great praise to Brian Boru. He continued to preach MacNeill's lesson of violence being only justifiable in the context of possible success, and by doing so, as Dr Fitzpatrick stresses, he repudiated the direct tradition of the Easter Rising as he would not have done had he 'urged cessation of bloodshed until a new generation had grown up unsanctified by carnage'. He had imposed a formal control instead of leaving matters to an ideological time-bomb. The many admirers across all party ranks felt after his victory in Clare, by the slashing majority of 5,010 to 2,035, that he must now come to terms with the political realities. He well knew that his East Clare achievement was partly based on a massive repudiation of old politics and that his surest way as a politician was still to be an anti-politician. He was urged by persons outside his movement to join the Irish Convention, set up by Lloyd George to comprehend all parties. He realized instinctively that his innocence must either disappear or destroy him in such a gathering, and that he would be tarnished by its bargaining. So he and his associates took their stand on the issue of a Republic. The tide was flowing in his direction. It was not necessarily flowing in the direction of a Republic. But a Republic formed an excellent excuse to stay away from what he did not want to enter. The Convention was the old politics, conducted before a vast audience. He could rely on its ineffectiveness, left to itself; and wishing as he did to replace it, as the custodian of the destinies of a future Ireland, he had no wish to rescue it. Accused of seeking to wreck it from the outside, he pleasantly replied that he had no need to do so, since Carson could be trusted to wreck it from the inside. It would not be the last time that Ulster, no less than the Republic, proved in his eyes the means of doing his work for him.[2] He signalled his real priorities in the victory speech in which he hailed America's probable reaction.

The East Clare election made de Valera and his movement respectable; it made him the leading standard-bearer of that movement; it also made politics respectable in the eyes of the movement. The next by-election was by curious coincidence the third caused by the death of an old Parnellite (the Parnellites were more radical, and decidedly more IRB in sympathy, than the anti-Parnellites before party reunification in 1900). W.T. Cosgrave took Kilkenny City on 10 August, but by 772 votes to 392, so there was no rival to de Valera here (as yet), although there was a warning that East Clare might not repeat itself on a national level. Then the most formidable alternative to him was eliminated, when Ashe, imprisoned for an incendiary speech, and having gone on hunger-strike, died of forcible feeding in Mountjoy Jail on 25 September. Ashe clearly was embarked on a course of more direct confrontation with the authorities: the IRB was likely to be apprehensive of too much success attaching to constitutional methods. Now de Valera, having commemorated Ashe in a dignified oration, was chosen a month later as President of Sinn Féin at its Árd-Fheis (Convention: literally, and pleasingly, High Festival). The founder, Arthur Griffith, and the first by-election victor, Count Plunkett, withdrew in his favour.

Here again the new politics was dictated by the symbolism of age: Griffith had been politically active for twenty years and the old Count had been a Parnellite candidate as far back as 1892. In his speech de Valera had to rationalize the way Sinn Féin had been made acceptable to the heirs of the Rising and their uncertainly-spanning spectrum of political allies.[3] His pragmatic Republic had a very interesting precedent in his native land. The United States had had its independence first, and devised its Constitution later. He stressed the inapplicability of the term 'constitutionalist' by denying the title of Britain to govern the people of Ireland, having received no consent to do so: a fine American revolutionary argument which would have won warm approval from John Adams. He wound up with a quotation from Henry Grattan, the most illustrious Protestant patriot of the Irish Parliament in the eighteenth century, in harmony with his use of the American revolution. Having taken over Griffith's post in the transformed Sinn Féin, he was chosen President of the Irish Volunteers in succession to MacNeill. Cathal Brugha, Ceannt's second-in-command at the South Dublin Union, became Chief of Staff, with Michael Collins as Director of Organization. Apart from de Valera and Brugha, the Volunteers were heavily under IRB control; Sinn Féin was not.

De Valera toured Ireland extensively in the next months, on behalf of both organizations. By-elections began to indicate some loss of momentum: the next three were in safe Unionist seats, and then the Irish Parliamentary Party began to regain ground. Armagh South went against Sinn Féin almost two to one on 2 February; Waterford elected John Redmond's son, a serving officer, after the death of his father, with a majority of five to three on 22 March; and Captain W.A. Redmond's old

seat in Tyrone East stayed with the old party by a majority of three to
two on 3 April. Catholic Ulster was not going Sinn Féin. But Lloyd
George restored the loss of Sinn Féin momentum by the threat of
military conscription for Ireland, and when the new Bill passed its third
reading on 16 April, the Irish Parliamentary Party under John Dillon left
the House of Commons to organize resistance. The Catholic hierarchy
met on 18 April and received Dillon, de Valera, the dissident
constitutionalist MP, Tim Healy, and the labour leader, William
O'Brien, together with the Lord Mayor of Dublin. It is important that de
Valera was very ready to make the most of this offer—this time the
advantages lay entirely with him. Dillon and his followers were not even
troubling to contest a by-election in Tullamore scheduled for 19 April.
Dillon was convinced that Lloyd George and his heavily Tory coalition
were greedily ready to see the Irish Party thrown to the dogs while
Ireland was torn to pieces by the extremists. In fact, Lloyd George was
unable to resist political pressure to force on Ireland the same treatment
as was being meted out to Britain. He clearly gambled on Dillon's people
losing caste while the new Sinn Féin could be tarred with the pro-German
brush and treated accordingly. But the Catholic hierarchy had no
intention of being outflanked in a political crisis which threatened its
control: the bishops had taken stock of de Valera: they found no Lenin
there. They would see their house stood on a strong foundation even if
Lloyd George was wantonly ready to sow the wind and reap the
whirlwind. They had been passive' enough even when the Pope had
spoken against the war: now they had a spiritual obligation to be passive
no longer. De Valera told them frankly that the Volunteers would fight if
conscription were enforced 'and they had no use for passive resistance'.
Cardinal Logue of Armagh answered: 'Well now, Mr de Valera, when I
talk about passive resistance, I don't mean we are to lie down and let
people walk over us'. The meeting accepted de Valera's draft of a pledge
to be taken by the people in every parish:

> Denying the right of the British Government to enforce compulsory service in
> this country, we pledge ourselves solemnly to one another to resist
> Conscription by the most effective means at our disposal.[4]

The campaign began under impeccable auspices, but in such a situation all
the advantages lay with de Valera as opposed to the old parliamentarians.
If that was not enough, Lloyd George obligingly made martyrs of the Sinn
Féin leadership once more. De Valera was arrested on 17 May, under the

Defence of the Realm Act, on suspicion of being involved in a plot with Germany, and was ultimately transported to Lincoln Gaol.

It is a symptom of how far the heirs of the Easter Rising had travelled from Pearse that a howl of rage greeted this fabrication. The valuable information that a brother-in-law of Sinéad de Valera found boating on Dublin Bay contrary to Admiralty regulations meant that de Valera was in contact with a German submarine, was regarded as a joke in indifferent taste. Seventy-three others were imprisoned at the same time as de Valera including Arthur Griffith, W.T Cosgrave, Count Plunkett and Countess Markiewicz. The first victims were the wretched Irish Nationalist Party, smashed three to two at the East Cavan by-election on 20 June by the candidacy of Griffith. As for Germany, it seems to have been generally agreed that it had callously used the Easter Rising to gain valuable propaganda advantages over Britain, and had taken good care that it would only be a noticeable source of martyrs. Certainly de Valera on the very eve of his arrest gave it no comfort at all. In an interview with the Boston *Christian Science Monitor* published two days before his arrest, he scouted the notion that an independent Ireland would hand over her ports to Germany:

> To be free means to be free, not to have a master. If England took away her troops and our independence were acknowledged, we would fight to the last man to maintain that independence. It is not a change of masters we want, though I do not know that the change would be for the worse.

It was a direct foretaste of his future foreign policy, which he never altered. Others among his associates might in the future be led into desire for alliance with Britain, Germany or the USA but never he. Nature had made him an internationalist in perspective, psychology a nationalist in conviction: he harmonized them all his life long.[5]

Conscription was never imposed on Ireland. But after the armistice Lloyd George's 'khaki' election of 14 December became in Ireland the anti-khaki election. If it seems perverse in the Irish to have used the election, regardless of the end of the war, as its best means for expressing its feeling on conscription—by the means of an overwhelming vote for one party which had opposed it as against another which had also opposed it—what is to be said of a Government which responded to the mandate for de Valera by keeping him and his followers in gaol for non-existent conspiracy with an enemy the Government was no longer fighting? It is not too much to say that because of this abysmal failure to respond to realities, many British and Irish lives were lost, British politics were poisoned for the life of an otherwise fairly effective government, and Irish history entered on a vicious spiral of violence whose longterm effects are still with us. Lloyd George has been vehemently attacked for doing much in relation to Ireland during his peacetime coalition government; but his greatest injury to it seems to have been that in December, 1918, he did nothing. In particular, he left critical moderate figures behind bars, while on the loose were still the organizer of genius, Michael Collins, and the implacable zealot for the Easter Republic unalloyed by pragmatism, Cathal Brugha. The situation was negotiable.[6] The revised electoral register under the 1918 Act had revolutionized Irish voting, the electorate having nearly trebled in size to reach a figure of almost two million, and the major cities being well above this. The Government was confronting—or rather failing to confront—a world unknown.

Sinn Féin won 73 out of the 105 seats, the Unionists 26 (23 in Ulster), the Irish Parliamentary party 6. De Valera was re-elected *in absentia* in East Clare without opposition, defeated John Dillon in East Mayo by a two to one majority, and was himself defeated by more than that in Belfast, Falls, where the Catholic population remained true to their old Redmondite leader, 'Wee Joe' Devlin. Before the election the Irish party had thrown in its hand in 25 seats such as East Clare, to the profit of Sinn Féin, but the major lessons to be learned come from Ulster. The Unionists contested and lost Donegal East, and Monaghan North, and left Cavan alone; otherwise, their Ulster effort was restricted to what is now Northern Ireland. They lost two seats in Tyrone but held Tyrone South by an overall majority. They lost Londonderry City to Eoin MacNeill but took both seats in the county. They narrowly held Fermanagh North but lost Fermanagh South. They won all seats in Antrim and two in Armagh but did not contest South Armagh. They won all seats in Belfast apart from Falls which they did not contest. They took four seats in Down and lost South Down. But it was also noteworthy that where the Catholic hierarchy's carve-up did not obtain, Irish Party candidates were normally ahead of Sinn Féin in the future Northern Ireland. (Tyrone South is the exception but the third candidate was not an official Irish Party candidate.) In sum, the Sinn Féin movement in eastern and central Ulster did not speak for either Protestant nor Catholic majorities. De Valera had to live with that political arithmetic, which he did by keeping the question as abstract as possible. Sinn Féin talked of refusing to allow secession in Ulster, citing Lincoln (the President, not the gaol); but this was bluff, and Lincoln had long been pressed into use by the enemies of Home Rule in British and Irish politics to the same effect.

Lloyd George and Bonar Law had issued a joint election manifesto which on Ireland had declared:

> . . . we regard it as a first object in British statesmanship to explore all practical paths towards the settlement of this grave and difficult question, on the basis of self-government. But there are two paths which are closed—the one leading to a complete severance of Ireland from the British Empire, and the other forcible submission of the six counties of Ulster to a Home Rule parliament against their will.[7]

Ulster has nine counties, but it is clear what was intended and it was reasonable enough: moreover the Ulster Catholic vote, had they troubled themselves about it, greatly strengthened their hand. On the other hand the assumption that the Sinn Féin victory in the 26 counties meant unacceptable intransigence invited exactly that. To embitter matters further, the Unionists in the 26 counties regarded the manifesto as betrayal. But Bonar Law's chequered career of defence of the Union had been for Ulster, not for all Ireland, and so had F.E. Smith's. Carson fought for a Unionist Ireland, but his lieutenant James Craig had not. In any event, Sinn Féin, true to Griffith's old abstentionist policy, now announced the calling of an all-Ireland assembly, to be known as Dáil Éireann, and summoned all the elected Irish MPs to its proceedings. It netted a total of 28, all from its own 73, the rest of whom were either in prison or in hiding. Under the Presidency of Cathal Brugha, who had sustained wounds in the Easter Rising so severe that his life had been presumed at its close, the Dáil announced its continuity in objective with the Easter insurgents and 'did ratify the establishment of the Irish Republic'. De Valera's legerdemain had made this possible, but he had also kept the Republic firmly as a base from which to negotiate. Simultaneously with the opening of Dáil Éireann and without its knowledge two policemen were shot dead when Volunteers under Sean Treacy and Dan Breen ambushed a cart containing gelignite. The Anglo-Irish war was on, and it was out of Sinn Féin civilian control from the start.[8]

The tendency of de Valera's conduct up to now had been very much against a violent confrontation, however vigorous his rhetoric as custodian of the Easter sacrifice. He had grasped the essential point that the Easter heroes had gained thousands by their martyrdom where their violence had only served to alienate. His extensive tours before imprisonment had been educational in arousing a people to non-violent protest against legislation of violence, which literally would have kidnapped them for service in a war they no longer saw as theirs. Psychologically, he wanted acceptance, and

East Clare had given it to him. He had a natural belief in the use of the democratic process, however British its origin; his American antecendents and analogies offered him a convenient, and natural, means of de-Anglicizing the democratic process in his own mind. Moreover, he wished to win the respect of the country in which his mother lived. This was tied nominally to the Peace Conference, but it was very largely the Americans of whom he and those he influenced were thinking when he spoke of the Peace Conference. On his release from imprisonment in 1917 he and the other officers had signed a statement to President Woodrow Wilson and the United States Congress stressing their martyrdom and the legitimacy of their national aspirations. It was chiefly his repudiation at the wartime by-election in South Armagh which elicited his most pointed hints at the use of force, with an unveiled implication that if the Unionists did not capitulate to Sinn Féin, they would be driven forth from the temple of Ireland. The 1918 General Election had involved his personal repudiation by the Catholics of West Belfast. In ensuing months in America he would explicitly ignore all of this, but would substitute in its place not a threat of coercion but a self-fulfilling prophecy of unity from conciliation. It was chimerical, and it showed an inability and unwillingness to come to terms with the already proven facts of his rejection in the North-east, but it also testified to his own alienation from the politics of the gun.[9]

Now, while he remained in Lincoln Gaol, the situation in Ireland was becoming increasingly intractable. He had used the rhetoric of the Republic to make the maximum use of the democratic process, but he could hope, left to himself, to make some inroads on seemingly intractable purists. He had drawn Brugha out of the IRB. He had compelled the acceptance of MacNeill by Sinn Féin and made short work of Countess Markiewicz when she objected. He played the politics of coalition, and performed the good missionary priest's work of encouraging the potential convert however dubious its previous spiritual record. For all of his absence from its establishment, the Dáil was the logical outcome from his methods.

Despite its occasionally sanguinary history, the IRB had its own traditions of non-violent gestures to rouse public opinion, the most famous being the rescue of its founder, James Stephens, from gaol on the eve of his trial in 1865. The process was now repeated as de Valera was spirited out of Lincoln Gaol through a series of steps including the temporary theft of the Catholic chaplain's key by his altar-server (de Valera), the use of sacred candlewax to provide impressions, the smuggling of several keys through cakes with initial lack of success, and the ultimate departure of the prisoner and his rescuer Harry Boland under the guise of a courting couple.

De Valera enjoyed the pleasure of seeing himself hailed in the press as the Houdini of his country. He gave a clandestine interview to an American journalist for the United Press news service, comparing Lloyd George to Machiavelli but placing his faith in the good judgement of the American people. Machiavelli, on his side, responded by releasing the other prisoners after de Valera had spent some weeks in hiding and indeed was on the verge of leaving for America. He returned to Dublin where on 1 April he was made President of Dáil Éireann, naming a cabinet in which Griffith had Home Affairs, Brugha Defence, Collins Finance, Count Plunkett Foreign Affairs, Cosgrave Local Government and Countess Markiewicz Labour. Labour itself, the heirs of Connolly, urgently needed conciliation, having given Sinn Féin a free hand in the 1918 Election; it was the opinion of informed observers that the vile slums of Dublin offered a natural basis to the transformation of the Irish crisis into a Bolshevik base. It remains a historical irony that the slums, which had most reason of any sector of Irish society to revolt, remained quiescent as the nationalist disaffection around them roared into a blaze.

But while de Valera had now made his name a household word, in Ireland at least, he was faced with a more complex problem of identity. Quite apart from the margin for error in his attempts to enshrine the Easter Rising by sealing it off in its own time and year, what he stood for differed vastly across the country. His people knew who was de Valera; they were divided on what was de Valera. His normal powers of being the good politician who touched widely contrasting potential sources of loyalty was now complicated by the de Valera who was cited in the seething plot of conflicting loyalties which constituted Irish politics and society in 1919. In the preceding General Election de Valera had hardly required a campaign in East Clare; but in West Clare the party managers had imposed a candidate, also elected without opposition, in the shape of Brian O'Higgins, who in the future largely divided his energies between the cults of Easter and Christmas, as furthered by appropriate valedictory cards and booklets. In East Mayo, the de Valera forces had whipped up opposition to John Dillon on the decidedly bourgeois, if highly American, cry of 'de Valera and no taxation'. In West Belfast, de Valera's cause was preached to the text 'Workers of the World Unite' although the Unionists responded by varying their normal coinage of anti-Catholic racism in allusions to him as 'a half-breed Spaniard'. As President of the Dáil, de Valera's eye on America was carefully attuned to the presumed American loyalties of

1918, as opposed to 1916 and even the more exotic features of 1776 or 1765. He was determined not to put a foot wrong in his overture to his native land.

He made it very clear that the form of approach to the Peace Conference was a very different one from that with which Ceannt beguiled his troops in the South Dublin Union in 1916. Then the intended approach was that of a belligerent power in alliance with Germany. Now Ireland was to be a suppliant inviting sympathy by analogy with Germany's most celebrated victim in Allied propaganda, Belgium. The Catholicism of both countries was promiscuously stressed in public references, with special emphasis on Cardinal Mercier. De Valera himself instructed Dáil Éireann on 10 April 1919 that Ireland must treat the British in the way Belgium had been told to treat its German conqueror:

> Our first duty as the elected Government of the Irish people, will be to make clear to the world the position in which Ireland now stands. There is in Ireland at this moment only one lawful authority, and that is the elected Government of the Irish Republic. Of the other power claiming authority we can say—adapting the words of Cardinal Mercier—'The authority of that power is no lawful authority. Therefore in soul and conscience the Irish people owe that authority neither respect, attachment, nor obedience. . . . Towards the persons of those who hold dominion among us, we shall conduct ourselves with all needful forbearance. We shall observe the rules they have laid upon us, so long as those rules do not violate our personal liberty, nor our conscience, nor our duty to our country.'
> . . . Such use of their laws as we shall make will be dictated solely by necessity and only in so far as we deem them to be for the public good.[10]

As to the politics of confrontation, de Valera introduced and carried a motion calling for ostracism of the Royal Irish Constabulary. This was to invoke the tradition of non-violence, going back to the preachment of boycott under Parnell and Davitt. There was still colder comfort for the heroes of Soloheadbeg on 8 April, when de Valera administered a characteristic invocation of Republican pieties to be rigorously tied in practice to the principle of civilian control by the democratically elected representatives. He was speaking as President of Sinn Féin, to which office he had been triumphantly re-elected at its Árd-Fheis:

> Regarding the Irish Volunteers, I have always held the same attitude as regards physical force. If I were a slave and if I had a stick, I would use that stick against the tyrant; I am not going to tie my hands behind my back . . .

Our last reserve is the Irish Volunteers. If the English Government were to keep me in gaol until such time as I would renounce the Irish Volunteers, then I would die in gaol.

The Irish Volunteers are now a national force at the disposal of the elected Government of the Irish people—they will obey that Government despite England's Army of Occupation—their attitude will be exactly that of the Belgians and the Belgian Government as defined by Cardinal Mercier.[11]

His timeliness was pointed enough. On the previous day, an attempted rescue of a Sinn Féin prisoner in Limerick, his Limerick, had resulted in the deaths of an RIC man and the prisoner himself. A month later two more RIC men were killed at Knocklong in the rescue of Seán Hogan. None of these had been planned killings, though Knocklong was a grim answer to de Valera. But on 23 June the assassination of District Inspector Hunt in the centre of Thurles without the slightest information given to the investigating police by the numerous witnesses, indicated that the gunmen had no intention of leaving their programme to be decided by Dáil Éireann. The Government responded by the usual official folly of clamping down on the possible forces of restraint within the nationalist movement, to say nothing of tying civilians and gunmen together in the public mind as well as in its own. It proclaimed all Sinn Féin organizations illegal in Tipperary, choosing for the purpose a date hardly likely to win it sympathy in the USA, the Fourth of July. On 10 September Sinn Féin was proclaimed an illegal body in Cork after an IRA attack on a church party of soldiers in Fermoy, and Dáil Éireann was proclaimed illegal throughout Ireland. De Valera had gone far in the demand for democratic control, and his plans were frittered to pieces by the real advocates of force on both sides. But since 11 June he himself had been in the United States, and he would be out of Ireland until 23 December 1920. He returned to find Ireland had become a slaughterhouse, ruled by terror and counter-terror.

Why did de Valera stay in the United States so long, and indeed why did he go at all? Only he had the credentials and authority to keep together the gunmen and politicians, it has been stressed, and certainly those he left in charge had little capacity for it along his methods of division between cult and service. Griffith, his deputy, had small stature among the heirs of Easter; MacNeill had relatively little and de Valera—perhaps to obscure his current intellectual obligations to the great historian—had not included him in his Cabinet; Brugha, both because and in spite of his rigidity, was caught between the IRB and the politicians without sympathy for either; Cosgrave's capabilities were unknown to himself and to others; Count Plunkett was a figurehead, and was apt to inspire in colleagues the readiness to think of others also as figureheads; Countess Markiewicz was widely, if affectionately, known as 'Cracked Madame'. Collins moved into the vacuum by becoming both gunman-in-chief and politician *par excellence,* but with none of de Valera's fastidiousness about keeping the cult of the former in the service of the latter. Collins simply took the offices he had and made them the means of control. As Minister for Finance he had to know about all the Cabinet transactions; as Director of Organization and later of Intelligence he had to know about all the Volunteers' transactions too. He became President of the IRB about the same time as he received the Dáil portfolio of Finance. Harry Boland, who had been sent initially on the mission to America, and remained there with de Valera, was one of his closest friends.

The ascendancy of Michael Collins, and the fantastic reputation he acquired as a folk-hero, all lay in the future when de Valera departed. Yet it was to the charming, rough-spoken, vigorous Corkman that de Valera himself naturally sent virtually his first letter from the USA: 'I have been trotting around—Rochester, Philadelphia, Washington, Boston, New York, back and forward and broke all my appointments'. The readiness to drop his normal austerity and even mock his belief in order conveys something of the response Collins's magic could induce in others. Harry Boland, on whom de Valera came more and more to rely in America, was at hand to foster the fullest of confidence in 'Mick'. Collins became a great guerrilla leader and became the darling of the de Valera household, consoling them for the absence of the Chief. It was indeed hard for the younger children to think of their father at all. Máirín remembered an overheard conversation between Brian and Ruairí: 'Who is Dev?' 'I think he's Mammy's Daddy'. But Collins was in and out with financial support, presents for the children, jokes and laughter, the big rough boy with the tender heart. 'I am very grateful to you, and I shall never forget all you always did for me', wrote Sinéad to him after the Treaty split had sundered him from her husband. 'I remain, Your friend always, Sinéad de Valera.' It would be easy to argue that de Valera's sacrifice of family life placed an intolerable strain on his marriage. It did not, because of the love between them and the total confidence he had in her; but as that letter to Collins reveals, for all her shyness and insistence on privacy, she was no self-abnegating affirmator who forgot her own personal convictions in response to the demands of politics. But he was sure of her, all the more because she was her own woman.[12]

It was another woman who drew him so emphatically to the United States, and one whom he had every reason not to be sure of at all. The word

'Rochester' at the head of his brief itinerary described to Collins is the clue. Catherine, Mrs Charles Wheelwright, lived at Rochester, New York. She had responded to the promptings of maternal interest when sentence of death and imprisonment for life had recalled him to her attention in the columns of the world press. She had made public demand of the President for his release, to no effect. De Valera had written her from Lincoln Gaol in November 1918:

> If America holds to the principles enunciated by her President during the war she will have a noble place in the history of nations—her sons will have every reason to be proud of their motherland.

This appeal to American maternity is all the more ironic in that his statements on Wilson show a profound optimism, in stark contrast to his habitual judgements on conventional politicians and in flagrant defiance of what he must have known of Wilson's contemptuous dismissal of his claims on American support during his own previous imprisonment. The letter was doubtless intended for public quotation, and indeed these extracts duly appeared in the programme of the Third Irish Race Convention in the USA. He would not have missed the utility of Wilson as a stick with which to beat his 'Associate' (whom Wilson refused to call his 'Ally'), Lloyd George:

> These principles too are the basis of true statecraft—a firm basis that will bear the stress of time—but will the President be able to get them accepted by others whose entry into the war was on motives less unselfish?

The first audience for this would, of course, be the prison censors, and he knew it:

> What an achievement should he succeed in getting established a common law for nations—resting on the will of the nations—making national duels as rare as duels between individual persons are at present: if that be truly his aim, may God steady his hand. To me it seemed that a complete victory for either side would have made it impossible almost.

This was written in the aftermath of Wilson's personal achievement of the armistice ending the First World War. It was also intended as a signal to the Americans that he had no intention of belittling their war effort, however much Irish-American supporters of the Easter Rising might have been hostile to it. But the first purpose of the letter was to reassert his need for psychological reunion with his mother.[13]

We cannot know what the reunion involved. Certainly he came back to her on the visit again and again. He spent Christmas with her in 1919. The reports of the visit speak of a coldly silent person who with a smile at once knowing and forbidding had long discouraged inquiries from neighbours about her elder son. Mary Bromage, who made a diligent American biographer's investigations, learned that 'There was no frivolity about her and even her sister and her sister's grown children stood in some awe of "Aunt Kate" '. She flatly declined to sit at the same table when visitors were present, even if it was but her own parish priest; she waited with classical virtue on the diners.

On the other hand, de Valera does seem to have made a friend on the journey in the shape of his half-brother whose voluntary exile from his family among the Redemptorists ironically paralleled de Valera's enforced exclusion. 'Uncle Charlie' had obtained fine social mileage from his famous stepson making the most of his non-existent personal relationship with the American-born revolutionary leader, the shadow of a gunman if ever there was one. Indeed Uncle Charlie may have made some talk of de Valera's joining them in America during a brief Wheelwright visit to Ireland in 1907, by which time any such ideas, whatever support Mrs Wheelwright may have given them, were a mockery of de Valera's lost childhood. No doubt, a qualified schoolteacher would have been a welcome supplement to the pension Uncle Charlie drew from his former employers. But now as then power clearly rested with the silent mother. Uncle Charlie had his measure of freedom: he remained in the Protestant faith until his death-bed, some years later, when his son Thomas firmly took charge of his eternal destiny. For all of the Englishman's enjoyment of the reflected glory of his step-son, allusions to the subjection of the Irish by the English must have sounded a little ironic to him.

It was in Boston that de Valera saw Father Wheelwright, whom he then brought to New York for his great reception at the Waldorf Astoria, and the vigour with which the Redemptorist had previously campaigned for his half-brother suggests that he may now have supplied him with very useful independent evidence of the state of feeling on public questions in the United States. Father Wheelwright is something of a *doppelgänger* as both son and priest—the de Valera who might have been. Certainly de Valera needed independent guidance, for the Irish-Americans who must form the nucleus of his campaign—though he followed Parnell's tactics in 1880 in seeking to make the most of the potential sympathy of non-Irish American public opinion—had their own views which were far from certain to coincide with the practical needs of de Valera and his new Ireland.

There were two other dramas to unfold, one above the other although from time to time conflicting with one another. The uppermost is the great success story. There were almost unbelievable demonstrations in his favour; he became the freeman of city after city; he received the honours of State Legislatures from the obvious Massachusetts to the unexpected Virginia; he campaigned coast to coast; he became an American celebrity. Below this there was an increasingly bitter and apparently destructive conflict against the Irish-American leadership of Judge Daniel F. Cohalan of Tammany Hall and the great Clan-na-Gael leader and perpetual conspirator for Irish Republicanism John Devoy. The controversy was the first real check to de Valera's leadership in the world of Irish nationalism, and it haunted both him and his critics ever afterwards. It would be the case of Cohalan and Devoy against him, when they condescended to rational argument, that he was ignorant of the United States, that he was brash, abrasive, dictatorial, intransigent, insensitive, offensive, factious, ungrateful, unstatesmanlike, unsound, psychotic, and a disaster to the cause he claimed to serve. He was simultaneously accused of seeking to injure the best interests of the United States and of the Irish Republic. He was condemned as being insufficiently rigorous in support of the Republic, and arrogantly Utopian in his insistence on supporting the Republic. He was declared to have attempted gross interference in the politics of the United States.

In fact, however fortuitous, his achievement in the controversy was masterly. De Valera's American sense contrasts with his parochialism in matters Irish of which Sean Ó Faoláin spoke, and with his almost wilful blindness on Ulster. In a shadowy way it had been a part of his mind for a very long time. American news would have meant far more to him than to others even as a child: Mother was there, and news of America was news of her. Daily newspapers in Ireland and Britain in his prime were much more detailed in their American news than is the case today: analysis might be much poorer. De Valera seems to have realized that interests in Ireland from the Easter Rising onwards had produced support from areas remote from prominent centres of Irish immigration: early voices in support of the new Irish nationalism came from the legislature of Nebraska, and Senator Ashurst of Arizona. In the great American West, Irish-Americans had often risen with much more ease and prominence than was to be found among the products of the ghettoes of Boston, New York and Philadelphia. Hence he knew from the first that Cohalan spoke for an old, and parochial, form of Northeastern Irish-American machine politics, in many ways outmoded in the Progressive era. Devoy was the revered patriarch of Irish-American nationalism still exercising much attention through his newspaper the *Gaelic-American* but assuming an old-style commitment to exile politics.

The era of reform found little in common with either: the system which had produced Cohalan was the system the Progressives wished to sweep away, and Devoy's American politics, which were vigorous, had from the first been conservative Republican. De Valera was welcomed on his tour by reformers who saw themselves as having reformed the precinct, reformed the ward, reformed the city, reformed the state, reformed the Congress, reformed the nation, and who were now interested in reforming the world. Wilson had raised their expectations of the latter in order to enter the First World War, and support for Irish freedom was a logical area in which to develop their interests. Activists in the Irish cause included many without a drop of Irish blood, and the many more newly rejoicing in rediscovery of forgotten ancestral links. Some of these reformers had accepted the war, and some had not; but few had common ground with Devoy and Cohalan, the opponents of war, unlike the proponents, believing a world of difference existed between being anti-war and pro-German. The stand of de Valera, as expressed in the Dáil on 11 April, had much more appeal for them. He spoke for Progressives who had opposed the war and Progressives who supported it but were against a revengeful peace:

> The people of America, enjoying liberty themselves, and having had to fight for it themselves against a dominating power, understand what liberty is. They had been long enough at the head of neutral nations before entering the war to be able to judge calmly what the war meant for the world and what a lasting peace would mean for the world. . . .
>
> We must try and save France from herself. If there is a peace imposed on Germany now, there will be a desire for revenge on the part of the German people later on. The new treaty will be violated like [that of 1871], and another war of revenge must surely follow. . . . It is for those who have suffered less to compose France and to try to save her from an act that would endanger her future. We are here on behalf of the Irish people, and we are quite ready to take our part in a League of Nations which has as its foundation equality and right among nations.[14]

De Valera was opposed to a League of Nations tied to a vindictive peace, but the idea of an open League attracted him from the first as containing potential for ultimate Irish international development. He perceived that a body of this nature gave a role to small powers otherwise left at the mercy of the international law of the jungle. It was fundamental to his longterm ideals, as well as to his immediate strategy, to take Woodrow Wilson's war aims more seriously than Wilson appeared to be taking them himself. It is to his credit that, conscious of making his first appearance before the world as 'the official head of the Republic established by the will of the Irish people, in accordance with the principle of self-determination',[15] (to quote his New York press statement of 23 June), he tried to formulate a foreign policy which would serve Ireland equally well after independence as before. This was not simply the President of an imaginary Republic articulating dreams to convey the impression he was or quickly would be the President of a real one. A man who sounded as if he believed in and was planning for the eventuality against which his bonds were issued invited more confidence than would a modest and self-confessed Utopian.

Those of Wilson's critics who had believed in his Fourteen Points, like the *New Republic,* could readily make the transition to hostility to the Versailles Treaty and its specific League without rejecting the original Wilsonian ideal. De Valera offered them a means of conserving their dreams despite the brutal injury they had sustained from reality, and this, too, would be a lifelong hallmark of his domestic as well as his foreign policies. He was also anxious not to alienate supporters of Wilson in general. He knew of the longstanding Irish-American commitment to the Democratic party, John Devoy notwithstanding, and he was careful to ensure he and his various fellow-envoys for 'the Republic' throughout the United States did as little as possible to offend Democratic feelings which were currently very sensitive. He tried to restrain Diarmuid Lynch, for instance, from attacking a pro-Wilson speech by Senator Tom Walsh of Montana which had been made to an Irish group asking support for Wilson's League. Walsh had been vigorous in urging Ireland on the attention of Wilson and the Peace Conference. That he had failed was no fault of his, and was to a great extent the fault of Cohalan who had managed to fix it in Wilson's mind that the Irish cause at Versailles was tied to the advancement in power and status of the Judge, a bitter enemy of Wilson's initial nomination, a pro-German during Wilson's administration, and now on the verge of orchestrating as large a bolt as he could influence from Wilson's Democratic party.

The same considerations apply to another of de Valera's stances, one in favour of *a* League though not *the* League, this time speaking in public, in Father Wheelwright's Boston:

> We want a just League of Nations, founded on the only basis on which it can be just—the equality of right among nations . . . A covenant for a League of Nations can be framed at Washington as well as Paris. Now is the time to frame it. It is not enough for you to destroy, you must build.[16]

What de Valera had perceived—and once more it is prophetic for his domestic policy then, and, after a break, later—was a vast middle-ground between the intransigent Wilson, steadily losing popularity throughout the country, and the 'irreconcilable' Senators who, despite their brilliant tactical victories to destroy the Treaty in the Senate, never amounted even to one-third of that body and were even less representative than Wilson in the USA as a whole. There were the pro-League Republicans like former President Taft and former Secretary of State Elihu Root, who were thinking of an American-built League; and the fruition of these hopes did find realization in Washington, DC, at the Naval Disarmament Conference at the outset of the Harding administration which stopped for ten years a battleship race then threatening the peace of the world. Similarly it was the assurance to the many who had supported Wilson that de Valera was not tied to those anxious to destroy the President and all for which he had ever stood.

For Devoy and Cohalan in fact represented a very dangerous cul-de-sac for the Irish campaign in America. They were tied to a candidate for the Republican Presidential nomination in the election of 1920, Senator Hiram Johnson of California, who was fundamentally isolationist. In opposing their machinations de Valera was rescuing the cause of Ireland in America from the embrace of essentially xenophobic anti-British forces which once in power would have closed the door on any diplomatic leverage on Ireland's behalf. Britain would simply have written an isolationist America off. As President, Hiram Johnson would have been resolutely against any adventure in Europe.

De Valera insisted on a Republican Party Presidential Convention plank in June 1920 which would demand recognition of the Irish Republic; Cohalan was asking for the more acceptable formula of recognition of the Irish right of self-determination. De Valera's plank was of course rejected, Cohalan's narrowly accepted. But de Valera's immediate indication that the Cohalan plank would be unacceptable meant that the Republicans dropped it in disgust, and the Democrats only needed to make polite noises of sympathy with the Irish while quietly shouldering de Valera at their Convention into the wings. The episode is usually written off as a major set-back. In fact, it comfortably freed the cause of moral and financial support for his cause from identification with any party or faction. Had the Cohalan plank been written into the platform, it would have been interpreted as a tactical victory for the Hiram Johnson forces at a time when they badly needed one, and one success at a Convention is infectious. The Democrats would never have countenanced any plank which might seem to repudiate Wilson, to whom their Presidential nominee made a pious pilgrimage the moment his Convention was over. Platform pledges for Irish self-determination would have fluttered away on the wind like the rest of the campaign brouhaha once the election was over.

De Valera had maintained the principle that Ireland was a factor in American politics to be operated in the interest of demands in Ireland, not of political adventures in America. He had done so at some cost. He had split the formal movement of support for his cause, but on any statesmanlike level he had no choice in the matter. To win, he had been obliged to play the card of the Irish Republic for all it was worth. This inevitably meant giving hostages to fortune, with results that would overtake politics in Ireland itself. But he had shown that he knew how well rigidity on the Republic could force his enemies into impossible situations, and that was a trick he would be tempted to try again. In one respect he had little alternative. His serious attempts to play the politics of coalition among the warring American political factions led him in a press statement from New York in early February 1920 to suggest that Britain's fears of security could be offset by an independent Ireland's co-operation in a British 'Monroe Doctrine' for the 'two neighbouring islands', ensuring that Ireland would never enter into treaties which would impair its independence or give a foothold to foreign powers inimical to Britain on Irish soil. The proposal was fully consonant with his concept of international neutrality. He cited the Platt Amendment then in force which bound Cuba to refrain from treaties with foreign powers or give them military, naval or colonization footholds. He also argued that a true League of Nations would involve commitments from all of its supporting powers 'to respect and defend the integrity and national independence of each other and guarantee it by the strength of the whole'. Again, this was to foreshadow the policies he would advocate when President of the Council of the League of Nations in 1932. The fury of Devoy and Cohalan at the suggestion partly arose from personal antipathy by now, partly from the further aid and comfort it gave to internationalism in the United States, and partly from their intention that in a future British-American war Ireland would be a safe ally for the United States. Once again, de Valera saw the danger. He had rejected the Pearse idea that Ireland would become a German satellite. He was now rejecting any suggestion that it might become a satellite for anyone else, including his own native country. Devoy and Cohalan, who were ready to commit it to both fates, responded by charging him with apostasy to the ideals of the Republic. His tactics at the Chicago Republican Convention, then, were also intended to show that he was not to be pushed by anyone into second place in fidelity to the Irish Republic. This would also prove an ominous precedent.

He had learned something else too. Cohalan was nothing to him before his arrival in America. But John Devoy, more than any other living man, seemed to enshrine the principle of age-old devotion to the ideal of Irish Republican nationalism. He had now met the aged idol, and discovered him to be a venomous, scurrilous, hate-filled monomaniac, a casualty perhaps of fifty years of the conspiracies and feuds of exile nationalist politics. It made de Valera very chary of symbolism he could not control. It intensified his suspicions of all forms of secret conspiracy, especially the IRB, hatched from the same egg as John Devoy. It toughened him against endless invective within Irish nationalism itself: Devoy spewed his apparently bottomless poison against de Valera in the columns of his *Gaelic-American,* and richly disseminated it against any who might support him. It brought home to him once more how isolated he was: Devoy and Cohalan attempted to stir up trouble for him in Ireland, and McCartan, whom he sent home to explain the Cuban allusion, must have reported to him that his action had been received very coldly by Count Plunkett, Countess Markiewicz and Cathal Brugha, but that Arthur Griffith and Michael Collins had loyally stood by him and compelled acceptance of his action. The cunning Devoy probably had some success later in stirring 'ambition on the part of Collins while arousing suspicion in the mind of de Valera',[17] when he publicly contrasted them to Collins's advantage. Collins gallantly repudiated the adulation in a private letter to Devoy, but the damage had been done to de Valera's confidence and the serpent may not have belittled him in vain to the increasingly powerful guerrilla leader. De Valera's natural instinct to trust nobody, which he had built up so well from his repudiation by his mother, was now powerfully reawakened in the land where he found her.

Up to this time de Valera's had been a very lonely but remarkably shielded life. If he had been solitary, he had been able to rely on protection from a succession of contrasting forces: Father Sheehy, the Holy Ghosts, the conventions of teaching, the forethought of Sinéad, Thomas MacDonagh, Boland's Mills, Dartmoor Prison, Lewes and Maidstone, the triumphant election campaign, the sanctity of martyrdom and success, the ceremony of public speaking, Lincoln Gaol, the Presidencies of Sinn Féin, of the Irish Volunteers, of the Cabinet of Dáil Éireann. After his initial weeks in America he discovered the horrors of internecine strife and manipulation: he had known of MacDermott's antics largely by hearsay, but this was the real thing. To the lack of psychological fulfilment within him, created by his mother, was now joined the sudden crumbling of what had been steadily, even gloriously, increasing reassurance from without. His aide Liam Mellows, victor of Galway East and Meath North in the 1918 Election, wrote Connolly's daughter Nora: 'He has seen through them . . . All conceit gone from him . . . since he discovered the conditions. Never saw a sicker man. Disillusionment isn't the word.' Mellows later remarked to another friend, 'if it were not such a crucial hour for Ireland nothing would be more pleasant than to show up the whole hideous structure that battens on the work and sacrifices of the people at home. How dare the old man talk of the "young men at home" in view of the treatment meted out to the young men who came over since 1916'.[18] But with their dependence on the cult of Irish patriots of past and present, they could never tell the truth about John Devoy.

De Valera's dependence in 'play-acting' increased. He even borrowed Devoy's use of deafness to make himself appear remote from unwanted questions, developed more of the technique of losing himself in points of detail, insisted more on protocol, learned to talk over unwanted contributions from others. He built defences not only against the present, but against the past in the shape of Devoy, and increasingly against the future too. He had already shown readiness to condition convenient belief against inconvenient fact, in the case of Ulster; he now began to make it a more habitual response. Again, his mother had originally driven him into the business of trying to believe what was not true, and not to believe what was. America retrained him to act out his part before roaring crowds.

He had to return to face a far more terrible Irish crisis than he had left, and he may well have left it partly for want of answers. Already in the United States he was giving evidence of his secret unhappiness with the resort to violence far and wide on the part of his beloved Volunteers, now also being termed 'the Irish Republican Army', or simply the IRA. Just as he had asserted his identification with the Volunteers before his departure by contemplating not their resort to warfare but his own death in devotion to their cause, now he responded to the death by hunger-strike of Terence MacSwiney and the impending execution of the eighteen-year-old Kevin Barry by calling not for revenge but

If God wills that the freedom of our country should thus come in our own rather than in the blood of our enemies, we too shall not hesitate at the price or shrink from the sacrifice, nor will those who come after us value less the heritage we shall thus have purchased for them. The glorious standard our comrades have set must be ours; and in this, the last, phase of Ireland's

struggle, to which it has been their privilege to lead the van, our motto must
be theirs, the motto of 'victory, liberty or death'![19]

The ease with which he moved among the models of Lincoln's Second
Inaugural and Patrick Henry's most famous speech testify receptivity to
American traditions. They reinforced the feeling that his American origins
and loyalties had engendered from the first. Most Irish revolutionaries of
his generation had a Britishness as well as an Irishness; de Valera was, and
remained, much more American than British, though more internationalist than either. Unlike his colleagues, as the future would show, he
had relatively little Britishness on which to draw, even after the manner of
Brugha who drew on it in reverse. Already the British were beginning to
become aware that in any deal that might be done, future arrangements
would be complicated by his nationality.

He returned in hiding aboard ship as he had come out (when rats ate his
clothes). His new organization, the American Association for the
Recognition of the Irish Republic, would have 700,000 members by the end
of 1921 (Cohalan would be left with 20,000 in his). In terms of finance, he
had collected five million dollars. He had obtained a devoted adherent in
Harry Boland, and another in Liam Mellows. He had also obtained a loss
which was in fact a gain: Diarmuid Lynch, victor of South-east Cork in the
1918 Election, had been a dangerous critic of him ever since Lewes, less
able than Ashe, more ready to challenge him than Ashe, and in general an
embodiment of much of what de Valera disliked about the IRB. Lynch had
been deported from Ireland for slaughtering pigs (as a patriotic duty to
prevent their consumption by the British); this was *ex officio* as Controller
of Food for Sinn Féin—he was also Director of Communications for the
Irish Volunteers. The British authorities intended to let the pigs' revenge
run a long time to ensure Lynch stayed out, although their insistence that
his name was Jeremiah hardly improved their control of the situation. In
any event, the Devoy controversy led Lynch to resign from Dáil Éireann in
disgust. De Valera did not know how Lynch would have influenced
individuals in the IRB against him, but probably suspected the worst,
almost certainly incorrectly: Collins seems to have been dry-eyed about
Lynch's departure, irrespective of whether his continued exile derived
from de Valera or the pigs. The faithful Harry Boland, in any case, went to
the IRB Supreme Council in Dublin in September, 1920, obtained no fresh
orders, and nevertheless returned to the United States announcing that the
IRB would now sever its historic links with the Devoy's Clan-na-Gael. For
good measure he proclaimed it in the public press, a new proceeding for the

IRB with a vengeance. De Valera was showing a capacity to use the IRB for his own purposes, however much he continued to dislike it.[20]

It may be asked why the British had not deported de Valera to the United States. They had no opportunity to do so between Lincoln Gaol and the opening of negotiations in Summer 1921: they *could* have opened deportation proceedings at the time of his release in June 1917 (anything earlier would have been looked on as clemency or weakness), but given that the release was part of a general attempt, if unduly belated, to acquire some goodwill for the Government, it would have soured the whole atmosphere. They might have tried it instead of putting him in Lincoln Gaol, but that would have involved bringing the German plot of 1918 under scrutiny in the chilly climate of legal proceedings, and so delicate a product of hothouse nurture would hardly have been up to it. On his arrival in America in 1919 de Valera was asked if he was an American citizen and answered: 'When I became a soldier of the Irish Republic I became a citizen of that Republic.'[21] As he had not gone to the US authorities at the age of 21 or thereafter and sworn his allegiance to the United States of America, he was technically not an American citizen and was a stateless person. The British authorities might have retorted that such might be the case, but that Sinéad de Valera before his court-martial, and Father Thomas and Mrs Catherine Wheelwright, during his stretch in Dartmoor, had pleaded that he was a United States citizen, and that an American status demanding mitigation but forbidding deportation was surely an attempt to have margarine on both sides of his prison bread. But they did not attempt deportation. His *pas-seul* between national status and national identity came to a sudden end when in early 1927 he demanded a passport from the Irish Free State, and obtained it, for the purpose of going to the United States to appear in a legal case on the remnant of his Republican bonds, to raise money for his new political party, Fianna Fáil, and to console his mother—and indeed see to her future—after the edifying demise of Uncle Charlie; his priorities were not necessarily in that order. This American journey, like its predecessor, was unwelcome to his colleagues. He had not up to that point recognized the Irish Free State, and this, and not his subsequent entry into its Dáil, was the occasion when he did so, although he continued officially to deny that he had until 1932.

He departed from America in December 1920 having enabled his mother to fulfil the American dream of seeing her son as President—indeed 'President of the Republic' was what he was normally called in the USA and, as F.S.L. Lyons so charmingly remarked, he 'did not deny the soft impeachment'.[22] It was not always a compliment—the American Legion,

standard-bearer of the forces of extreme reaction which would have kept in
step with a Hiram Johnson isolationism, had declared

> the public reception of Emilio De Valera, an American citizen, calling
> himself President of the Irish Republic, is an insult to the men who were in the
> service of the United States, and is a reflection on the cause of which our
> comrades fought and died.[23]

It also made him a curiously senior figure, for all of his mere 38 years: after
all, the office was one of the symbolic father of his people, in American
usage, surrogate king as well as surrogate Prime Minister. Little objection
had been raised to his elevation in style, but the more regal the status, the
less might be the power. And if he was king, he was throughout 1920 king
over the water: it is a startling point that in his thinking the departure from
America was premature. His psychological need to exhibit himself in glory
in front of his mother, and his absorption in the increasing work of
maintaining American moral and financial assistance and driving Cohalan
and (surreptitiously) Devoy out of the temple of Irish nationalism began to
become the main business of his life.

What recalled him to his duties as father of his family and his country
was the news that Arthur Griffith had been arrested. Michael Collins was
now Acting Acting President, in addition to his seemingly endless number
of other jobs, which meant that the headship of state and the prosecution
of the war were incarnate in the same man. The situation was even more in
Collins's hands than this would indicate: his quickfire decision prowess
and his towering contempt for inefficiency had effectively given him the
initiative as well as infuriating the Minister for Defence, Cathal Brugha,
and the Minister for Justice, Austin Stack.

Éamon de Valera returned to find himself forced to assert real authority.
He had to act the part of father in his home, in contrast to the somewhat
boisterous conviviality Collins had imposed, and in his visits continued to
inject. De Valera had never known a father, and his treatment of his
children while meaning to be kind, had the insistence on discipline which he
associated with fatherhood: his will must be supreme, just as he had made
MacDonagh's supreme over him. He wanted to make the same provision in
politics, and this did not so much place him in opposition to Collins, as to
Collins's programme of violence. The whole tendency of his campaign in
America had been to see Ireland as victim, not fighter. He was resolute on
Ireland's right to be a Republic, but his plea was one of aid for the sufferer,
more than of support for the effective guerrilla. His was, so to speak, the
church of the martyrs. Collins used everything from assassination of key

British intelligence officers in front of their wives to the hunger-strike and lingering death of Terence MacSwiney and the police murder of his predecessor as Lord Mayor of Cork, Tomás Mac Curtain. But his enthusiasm for martyrs was entirely limited to their propaganda value. He privately admitted that he would have had no use for Pearse had he realized his essential objective was the dream of martyrdom; he admired Austin Stack as the suffering organizer of prison protests, but he was incapable of allowing this to offset his detestation for Stack's subsequent bungling as a Minister. De Valera, then and later, was far more ready to acknowledge martyrdom as a credential for office outweighing personal inadequacy. Basically Collins saw the Volunteers in terms of attack, de Valera saw them in terms of defence. His American mission was many things, but the least of these, insofar as it existed at all, was an apostleship for 'freedom fighters'.

His solution to the problem of violence and Collins was characteristic: he proposed that Collins take over the American mission. Collins's IRB had not backed Harry Boland to the final limit of a new Clan-na-Gael: if he went there himself, de Valera believed he would think differently. De Valera may even have been thinking of the climate of American opinion with respect to war. The Americans wanted to honour their war dead, but they were in revulsion against the idea of war in general and Harding's election was a repudiation of the gospel of war and the Government crusade fostering suspicion and repression of radicals which had accompanied the war and for a time accelerated after it. De Valera himself seems to have been influenced by the farewell to arms. He may have felt that Collins would be educated by the experience, as he had been, and gain a different perspective as a result. It is certain that his offer to Collins was a sign of trust at this stage: the struggle against Devoy and Cohalan had meant far too much to him for his anxiety to send Collins over to be anything but the entrusting of his American honour to a friend in whom he had the utmost confidence. But the proposal foundered, Collins remarking affectionately that 'the long whoor' (a Cork term of endearment) would not get rid of him as quickly as that.

This setback for de Valera was the precursor to seven grim years of failure on his part to control the gunmen. His psychological hunger for acceptance made the failure hard to contemplate, much less admit: and his role in public as he conceived it ruled out any question of admitting his fallibility. Hence when, time and again, before and after the Treaty and the Civil War, he was swept aside by the gunmen's logic, he had to go through motions that the repudiation had been no repudiation, he could no more admit that he was struggling against the gunmen than he could call into question the Republican tradition despite the proof of its uglier face so graphically presented by John Devoy. He made an attempt to convince the Dáil early in 1921 that activities which had the look of murder should be given up; he got nowhere, and dropped it. He had evidence, although he may not have known it, that non-violent action was working. The Sinn Féin courts had proved remarkably successful, even popular with the otherwise alienated Unionist population in the South. Cosgrave and his assistant in Local Government Kevin O'Higgins had operated so skilfully that at the Local Government elections of January and June 1920 Sinn Féin won a landslide, and persuaded all local councils outside Northeastern Ulster to break with the British Government's ministry, the Local Government Board, for all the grim financial risks this entailed. But de Valera was very slow to recognize the significance of Cosgrave and his achievements. Of course he kept Cosgrave on when he later redeployed his Ministers: in August 1921 he put Count Plunkett in a post outside the Cabinet, he put Countess Markiewicz's post outside the Cabinet—they had criticized his moderation, and their demotion was not likely to cause controversy. Brugha's would have been.

De Valera's hand was in fact very weak on the issue of violence. The British had both Griffith and MacNeill behind bars, as well as several other moderates. Griffith had a good record of non-violence, even if he had wavered at Easter Week: MacDermott is said to have told him to go home. He had deferred to Collins's force and charm, but his natural instincts would probably have led him to support de Valera's qualms, once he had a sufficiently powerful force giving him a lead, for like many a bully Griffith needed a support-figure. Another casualty to the prison authorities was de Valera's former co-enchainee, the Imagist Desmond FitzGerald, who had been a brilliant and most effective Director of Propaganda. De Valera's recent work would have harmonized with FitzGerald's need to arouse as much sympathy for Ireland as possible. In his place de Valera chose a very obvious candidate—the converted English Liberal Erskine Childers who would have a fine range of contacts in British journalism to match those acquired by the engaging FitzGerald. Collins introduced them. It was to be important. Childers, like Brugha, needed intransigent devotion to the Republic to prove to himself and others that his mixed Irish and British origin made for no backsliding on his part, and he had an intellect far beyond poor Brugha. It played a part in hardening de Valera in the direction of the Republic as principle as well as tactic in the days to come. Certainly the fear Childers later excited among his Irish enemies is testimony to the recognition that a change had taken place following his presence, and it was in de Valera that change was most obvious. Griffith, who had shown genuine self-denial in standing aside for de Valera even in his own Sinn Féin, and who had been generous in the way he had done it, would see his own hopes of success through influence on de Valera frittered away, and was reduced in the end to snarling about the 'damned Englishman'.

Yet in early 1921 it seemed that, if conflict was to come at all between de Valera and Collins, it would be with de Valera for a cessation of violence, Collins against. Nor was Collins fully master of the situation. Local activity was still inclined to proceed on its own momentum. (When the crunch came in December 1921 and Collins opted for the Treaty with Britain, he proved unable to control his rural following.) Meanwhile de Valera responded to his own impotence in the business of restraining the gunmen by retreating into the position of a 'reigning' President, coming out with suggestions that Ministers should try to arrange for the writing of the histories of their Departments under Dáil Éireann. The response of the good-natured 'Mick' to this reveals the slightly amused affection with which he regarded the 'Chief': a fine, symbolic figure, scholarly and somewhat out of touch with reality. The Chief was a great man—but not really *au fait* with down-to-earth questions like the Anglo-Irish war and the way to talk to children. On the other hand Collins was much more tolerant of de Valera's hopes for negotiation than was Brugha, even if he had no intention of creating the climate for them by the suspension of military action. When they happened, he agreed to a truce, but not until then.

Then came the breakthrough. Lloyd George performed a *volte-face*. Negotiations were on. De Valera was arrested in June, and hastily released. The great bulk of Sinn Féin prisoners were released. De Valera met with Southern Unionists and then with Macready. After much exchange of firm assertions on both sides, de Valera and Lloyd George met. Lloyd George subsequently stated that negotiating with de Valera was like trying to pick up mercury with a fork, on being told of which de Valera, with all of the delight of a man from the plains for once having the laugh on a quick 'mountainy' man, inquired 'why doesn't he use a spoon?' In fact, de Valera had entered the negotiations with some very real problems of representation and accountability. Abstract formulae such as the inviolability of a Republic consisting of the Island of Ireland in its entirety, wholly independent of Britain, were fine as a base line whence to begin and to which to retreat, but it was clear that this was not a serious possibility as a target for British, and still less for Ulster Protestant, acceptance. De Valera had to work out how much he could concede without rendering his gains worthless; but he had also to measure how much he would be permitted by his following to concede.

He started from a position mathematically at the extreme point from a fully integrated Union (and in any case, given the presence of a separate Irish administration in Dublin Castle controlled from London ever since the Union's enactment, there never had been a fully integrated Union, a root-cause of its mortal illness). He differed from the old constitutionalists, and many of his own colleagues, in seeking a measure which would go as near as possible to the limit; he was at the limit himself, not being a part of the Union, and hence the Ireland he conceived as his spiritual female progenitor must be where he was. De Valera and his fellow ex-prisoners were probably much clearer about what they meant by freedom than were their British opponents who—apart from a brief experience of Winston Churchill's—had not the advantage of gaol. Freedom translated from their own experience into Ireland's meant the ability to control and direct its conduct and course of action, subject to certain restraints which might govern a free person towards society in general and towards a difficult but powerful neighbour in particular. The absence of freedom was living a life controlled by outside forces and being under forms of dictation, as their lives in gaol had been.

There remained the gunmen, or Volunteers. There was the British militaristic ideal in which they had all grown up, carrying with it the fear that their 'manhood' would be impaired by a compromise peace which implied their inability to win to the full. Many of them were not democrats at all, as we know the term. To them the act of taking up arms gave them a right to make the final decision. They had been very late in being brought even nominally under Dáil direction, and Collins's effective, but peculiar, methods of command had increased their feeling that matters were in their hands. They had constructively rejected the British blunder of formal war to go into guerrilla activity; many of them were as contemptuous of the British readiness to count the soldiers out in the final settlement. Besides, their whole existence had begun with a British example of military refusal to take civilian dictation with the Curragh mutiny of 1914. Carson's army had been staffed with some of the most eminent military figures of the day. Hence the Irish military acquiesced uneasily, insofar as they acquiesced at all, in civilian dictation, and after the split on the Treaty the military on both sides were to show their sense of superiority to the civilians down to the mutiny which threatened Cosgrave's rule in 1924.

As far as de Valera was concerned he had been so far out of touch that his acquaintance with the Volunteers in 1921 proved a new, and apparently pleasurably thrilling, experience.He had met the famous General, Tom Barry, on 23 May, and they were charmed with one another. As quasi-king he knew the rules of not saying anything which might seem to demean the struggle of the men nominally under his command, and asked in detail about the Volunteers' chances of continuing to hold out. Barry was left with the feeling that he was, in fact, anxious to continue the struggle, but was careful to exaggerate the advantages of his troops' situation in response to de Valera's enquiries. De Valera was concerned about the attitude of the people, and questioned how far they wanted to persist with the struggle. Barry, thinking professionally, interpreted this as relating to popular cover of Volunteer activities. In any case he thought enquiries about the people quite unimportant: it was the resolution of the soldiers that was the important thing.[24] De Valera's anxiety to protect himself by the use of ambiguities was beginning to tell against him: he clearly wanted Barry to think about questions like popular disenchantment and his own possible military weakness, but all he got was a gallant military affirmation that all was well. Such meetings may have given de Valera a temporary enthusiasm for the militarist position which because of its novelty and his previous lack of encounter with the Volunteers in their heyday could have had some affect in marginally hardening his attitude on negotiations. After his talks with Lloyd George he began to make references to spinning out the diplomacy in order to strengthen his troops' hand in a resumption of the war.

But his principal negotiating tactic can best be expressed by an adaptation of a phrase of Conan Doyle's, an author who could bring tears to his eyes. It was Sherlock Holmes's principle that when you omit the impossible, whatever remains however improbable, must be true. De Valera consistently demanded the impossible, and then made what he could of negotiation when that situation proved intractable. He had argued for the presentation of Ireland's case for recognition to the Peace Conference: the prospects were hopeless, but they cleared the way for an appeal to America. He sought recognition of the Republic in America: he could not get it, but he got a great deal, and disposed of much that was in his way, while pressing for it. He frankly told a secret session of the Dáil on 18 August that he 'himself would refuse to recognize it, if it could be imagined that he was elected President of the United States, because the American people would not back him and would turn him down at once if he dared to do it'.[25] Yet he had made his campaign in America supposedly on the point. After talking to Lloyd George, he apparently became clearer on what he was going to seek while keeping the discussion so rigidly around a Republic. He produced the doctrine of external association with the Commonwealth and put it to his Cabinet.[26]

External Association was far from a chimerical idea. George VI's biographer, Sir John Wheeler-Bennett, pays a handsome tribute to it, as a pathfinding proposal for Commonwealth relations. The King would be recognized as head of the Commonwealth. The proposal was firmly in line with Woodrow Wilson's insistence during the war on the USA's not being an ally of Britain, but an 'associated power', which, to de Valera's delight, had enabled him to negotiate the armistice with a free hand. It is evident that de Valera was still thinking American to considerable purpose, and also, as the statement to the Dáil secret session shows, that he identified his (now official) position as 'President of the Irish Republic' to some degree with that of the President of the United States. But he may also have had Wilson in mind in another respect. He knew, none better, that Wilson was felt to have lost much by going to the Peace Conference in person, where his influence would have been much greater, it was believed, had he only sent envoys. This surely had a great deal to do with de Valera's conviction that treaty negotiations with Lloyd George and his advisers should be carried out by a team consisting of Griffith, Collins, Robert Barton (his Minister for Agriculture and cousin of Childers), and two non-Ministers George Gavan Duffy and Éamonn Duggan. Cosgrave in particular protested against this removal of de Valera's formidable presence from a team clearly about to face the finest negotiators Lloyd George could field. De Valera was obdurate. Terence de Vere White, biographer of the pro-Treaty Kevin O'Higgins, told me that he suspected de Valera's intention was that the talks would deadlock, and he himself would then arrive as *deus ex machina,* resolving the *impasse.* This again was what Wilson's critics felt he should have done. It would also account for the diminution of importance of External Association in the making of plans if de Valera was reserving the real strength of his argument—including its value for the British themselves in their own Commonwealth relations in the future—for his own arrival.

In the event, the Treaty was accepted by the negotiators, ruling out External Association, demanding an oath to the King for elected representatives of the future Irish parliament, and confirming the *status quo* on the newly-formed substate of Northern Ireland which had come into being for the six northeastern counties under the Government of Ireland Act of 1920. A Boundary Commission was to resolve any anomalies in the future. De Valera was thunderstruck, and quickly moved into a position of hostility to the Treaty. He spoke of demanding the Ministers' resignations. But, apparently somewhat to his surprise, the Cabinet split against him when Cosgrave firmly backed the envoys. It then went to the Dáil for ratification. Many deputies doubted whether they could approve a measure which denied the continuation of the Republic, whose Dáil they constituted. It was here that the penalty was being paid for de Valera's public readiness to accept Brugha's initial insistence that the people in 1918 had voted for the Republic. To strengthen his own hand in the United States, de Valera had made a great point of it. But it was not true. In May 1921 under the Government of Ireland Act 1920 elections had been held for the Northern Ireland and for the unacceptable 'Southern Ireland' parliament whose assembly the Sinn Féin deputies would boycott but whose election mechanism they used to get themselves a second Dáil. Their candidates were returned unopposed in all seats save the four for Dublin University which was the last bastion of Southern Unionism. Hence there had been no time when the people had given a mandate for the Republic, save insofar as they had not opposed its representatives in 1921 with nothing else on offer. There would have been grave personal danger for anyone attempting such opposition. In the Dáil debates of December 1921 and January 1922 it was a parliamentary exercise that decided; and it was unanswerable that if the Dáil's relationship to the Republic gave the deputies no choice it was wholly improper to hold it at all. By taking part in it, all deputies acknowledged that the question was open, albeit many continued to argue that it was closed.

The great irony of the whole debate lay in the lack of emphasis on Northern Ireland. The Dáil was opposed to Ireland's partition: so were the Catholic hierarchy, and indeed this had been a major reason for many of them turning away from the Redmondites whom they had seen as insufficiently intransigent on the issue. It had been de Valera who had pledged in August that Sinn Féin would not use force to settle the Ulster question. He had stressed that it must be settled; he had told his initial New York audience that Ulster exclusion could no more be considered than that the Americans of 1783 could have considered the truncation of their territory by the Loyalists (that the Loyalists actually did in many cases maintain an American residence where there was still British North America apparently eluded him). He met with Sir James Craig, and talked about Irish history to the weariness of the Edinburgh-educated Ulsterman. But it is clear that this was a tactic of de Valera's both now and later—he also played it with Lloyd George—when he was unclear as how best to proceed. Significantly when de Valera was advising the Treaty negotiators on how to proceed if the settlement offered was unsatisfactory, he said they should break on Ulster. There would be odium attaching to whichever party broke off the talks: Ulster would be an acceptable excuse. But the Boundary Commission closed that door. By now the Catholic hierarchy were so anxious for peace that their objections to partition has become much more muted also. And in the Treaty debates as Maureen Wall said:

> Critics of the treaty concentrated on the crown, the oath and the empire, for the most part, and several of those who did make a fleeting reference to the Northern Ireland question, were concerned not with the loss of the six counties, but rather with the fact that this part of Ireland could provide a bridgehead when Britain decided to re-establish her rule in Ireland. Indeed document number 2—the alternative proposal put forward by Mr de Valera—showed no alteration in the articles relating to Northern Ireland, and seems to indicate that President de Valera had been convinced by the delegates that the Boundary Commission would solve the problem of partition.[27]

In a word, Northern Ireland also had become one of the 'impossibles' of which the most was to be made, when it could be made, in order to increase the leverage on other matters. This would remain de Valera's standard method for dealing with unwanted but popular proposals in domestic or foreign policy after his return to power in 1932: X or Y would be described as eminently desirable, but impossible with the existence of partition. There was a very strong contrast in the Dáil Treaty debates, as previously, between his own position and that of his devoted follower, the Belfast Catholic Seán MacEntee. MacEntee had accompanied de Valera in his speaking campaign of Winter 1917–18 and, as Dr John Bowman points out in his invaluable *De Valera and the Ulster Question,* talked of winning the Republic in twelve months where de Valera was admitting it might take forty years to convince all the Irish people including Ulster. In the Dáil debates MacEntee grimly predicted:

> Mark my words, under this Treaty Ulster will become England's fortress in Ireland—a fortress as impregnable as Gibraltar, and a fortress that shall dominate and control Ireland even as Gibraltar controls the Mediterranean. I have heard much from those who will vote for it because it is not a final settlement. I have heard much of our gradual growth to freedom under this instrument—how we will encroach a little here and crawl a little there until we attain the full measure of our liberties. I tell you that so long as Ulster is in the position you are going to place her in under this instrument you will not budge one inch.[28]

Even there, and it is the one major anti-Treaty speech dealing with Ulster, MacEntee linked his very understandable concern for his Ulster co-religionists with the chimera of Northern Ireland's use to overawe the rest of the country. It was as though to plead the cause of his own place of origin, he had to clothe it in terms which might elicit interest from an audience which clearly was not going to put itself out for the Northern Ireland Catholics and their uncertain nationalist loyalties. As for MacNeill, he had bitterly opposed the Dáil boycott of Belfast products as liable to alienate the Ulster Protestants beyond all hope: he certainly did not think Ulster a reasonable ground for opposing the Treaty now, and he accepted it. He did believe in the Boundary Commission, and would resign as delegate to it in 1925 with bitter mortification when it became clear that any change it might recommend would be to the territorial advantage of Northern Ireland.

There has been surprise at the way in which Collins, de Valera and friends and enemies of the Treaty alike placed so much faith in the Boundary Commission. It seems to me that it offered a convenient means of postponing a question with which Sinn Féin had never come to realistic terms. De Valera himself, never saw the inhabitants of Northern Ireland as part of the 'Irish people' whom he felt he understood so well; he had known Limerick, Tipperary and the Connacht Gaeltacht (Irish-speaking area) intimately as he was growing up and he later added strong personal knowledge of Clare, Dublin (despite his lifelong reservations about it) and the coastline and mountainous regions in which his support was strongest. Apart from brief visits in 1917–18, and a fugitive experience in 1924 and another in 1929 each of which cost him a month in a Northern Ireland gaol, he never knew the land that has been Northern Ireland since 1920. He enjoyed sending a Christmas card every year to his prison Governor in the Crumlin Road Gaol in Belfast, but that was his most tangible link with majority opinion in the substate.

His opposition to the Treaty was essentially on other grounds, and while these were deeply concerned with Republican symbolism, they were, like so much of the Irish-American view of politics, ultimately concerned with power. The question of the oath sounds an insane one for the Dáil to have debated so much, and for the country to have been plunged in a civil war. There was a doctrinal question about the oath, whether it did not involve perjury in that it abrogated previously-existing oaths to the Dáil itself and to the Republic (where these had in fact been sworn). But this was not a serious obstacle in his case. He had without scruple or ceremony abrogated his allegiance to the IRB despite having been sworn in by MacDonagh.

There was a question of dignity about it: forcing the elected representatives to take the oath had a flavour of a defeated army being forced to pass under the yoke in Roman days. One of his prizes at Blackrock had been Walter Scott's *The Lady of the Lake* and he would have been well acquainted with the famous line of its companion *Marmion* 'The hand of Douglas in his own.' The oath was a compulsory requirement of what should only be given voluntarily. He was President of the Republic; as such, he had infuriated British opinion in questioning the right of George V to reply to the good wishes of the Pope on behalf of the Treaty conference. Was he now to doff his proud Presidency and admit subordination to him with whom he had so recently claimed equality, if not (from the point of view of fidelity to the spiritual authority of the Pope) superiority? He had borne himself as President before the eyes of the world, of his native land, and of his mother. It was a terrible surrender to make, and he was not going easily to make it.

The oath was worrying on another ground. It was offensive to loyal Unionists to see the king insulted by persons being forced to take an oath to him which they did not wish to take. The king's glory was enhanced by the loyalty of his subjects, not by their enforced protestation. Did Lloyd George need so empty a triumph to convince his critics? His negotiators were presumably representative of Unionist opinion: did they believe in such a thing, and would they not have been able to convince their followers it was unnecessary? In the event, it seems to have deepened the anger of those who opposed the idea of a settlement. Carson still raged; Lord Alfred Douglas still declaimed:

> Who crawled to Collins like a mongrel cur?
> Who handed Ireland to a murderer?
> And gave His Feebleness dishonour's slur?[29]

De Valera may not have thought the thing through to this extent, but the question that concerned him, as it concerned MacEntee and so many of his supporters, was the thought that the oath symbolized a limitation of power so absolute that freedom was impossibly abridged by it. We now know that Collins's insistence on the whole settlement as a stepping-stone to greater independence was to be proved true, and that first FitzGerald and McGilligan as Foreign Ministers under Cosgrave, and subsequently de Valera himself when in power, would prove as much. But the oath sounded not only demeaning but alarming. It was attacked in theological terms; but much of the theology existed because of the alarm.

De Valera was to be violently attacked because of his opposition to the

Treaty. It seemed self-interested, and it was. It did not have the merit of coming from unbending Republicanism, as was acknowledged for Brugha and Stack (although detestation of Collins lent wings to the fury of both). Document No. 2 looked like a self-important irrelevance, all the more because it was somewhat petulantly thrust in and out of the discussion. Yet de Valera had a principle of significance here, although he was sadly perplexed as to how to handle his document which was based on original intentions of its disclosure not in Dublin, but in London. He would have been thinking of the Versailles Treaty fight in the US Senate, and of the powers of that body to amend. An amending process employed in the Dáil would in itself have forced a recognition of sovereignty and given an earnest that the power originally claimed had won acceptance, although resulting in something less than a Republic. But the situation grew quickly beyond him, and just as he had earlier retreated from his public doubts about a military solution, he now realized Document No. 2 must divide him from the bulk of anti-Treaty sentiment.

His pro-Treaty critics assumed he would have carried a large number of followers with him, had he put his pride in his pocket and accepted the Treaty. There is no reason to agree without question that they were right. Even MacEntee, for all of his future fidelity, had his lonely Ulster reasons for opposition to the Treaty which were independent of de Valera's manoeuvres. Brugha and Stack had been suspicious of negotiations, and if they had less personal reason to break from de Valera than from Collins, they would have been all the more anxious to show that it was principled and not personal reactions which animated them. The retention of approval by maternal figures was psychologically a crucial factor. Mrs Pearse just might have been able to follow his lead to vote for the Treaty. Mrs Clarke would not have done. And the younger women—Countess Markiewicz, Dr Ada English, Michael O'Callaghan's widow, and Mary MacSwiney, would not have done. The pro-Treaty feeling was as bitter as it was, subsequently, because of its supporters' awareness of their regard for him, which in the case of some of them—Liam de Róiste, Peter Paul Galligan, Robert Barton, his old Rockwell colleague Tom O'Donnell— led them to vote for or abstain on his re-election as President having just voted against him on the Treaty. Despite his own refusal to vote he was in some danger of being re-elected. Many more would have voted for him had they not realized the lunacy of having a President mandated to implement a Treaty he had so strongly opposed. Realizing, then, how powerful his reputation remained in their own ranks the pro-Treaty deputies assumed it swayed many persons against the Treaty. In the Dáil it probably did not. In the country it probably did. In the IRA it certainly did not. The Civil War would have happened if he had supported the Treaty, especially when one considers how independent of him were such major leaders on the anti-Treaty side as Liam Lynch and Rory O'Connor. He might have made the difference with personal friends like Harry Boland; it was enough heartbreak for Harry to oppose his beloved Mick. But the realities were set forth in the speech of Cathal Brugha, who in replying to Fionán Lynch's statement that he spoke for his constituency, said contemptuously:

> I had in my pocket a document signed by people who are entitled to speak for the young men, the fighting men, the men who count and who are ready to make sacrifices in his constituency, and that is the . . . two Brigade Commandants that cover the area in which his constituency is in. In this they say very respectfully to the Government that they are absolutely against the Treaty.

In a word, the future lay with the officers of the IRA whose men and whose civilian population counted as little as would the men and the civilian population in an area under British military control. It was left for de Valera to become the prisoner of the intransigent Republicans. The Dáil majority for the Treaty was 64 to 57. De Valera said that the Irish people had to disestablish the Republic before it could pass out of being. Michael Collins, fraught with chivalry and anxiety, cried impulsively that de Valera 'has exactly the same position in my heart now as he always had'. Mary MacSwiney leaped to her feet and in a furious speech declared 'this is the grossest act of betrayal that Ireland has ever endured'. Collins, knowing far better than de Valera the dangers ahead from the 'invisible' army he had once controlled, begged that the two sides come together to preserve order in the country. But de Valera, all his realism gone, in the utter destruction of the power and acceptance that had put to flight those ancient ghosts of isolation and rejection, cried out 'The world is looking at us now—' only to collapse in hopeless, cruel weeping. It may have prefigured a period of something very close to psychological breakdown, and the desperation of his speeches in subsequent months suggests as much.

Brugha, icy, controlled, righteous, answered them all: 'So far as I am concerned I will see, at any rate, that discipline is kept in the army.'[30]

4

The Ice

From old Brid they heard about the giant that stole the king's crown but were never told how it was found again.

—Sinéad de Valera, 'The Stolen Crown'

...for reign, *read* rein.

—John P. O'Carroll and John A. Murphy,
erratum correction, *De Valera
and his Times*

The army killed Brugha on 3 July 1922, although it took him two days to die. It took Harry Boland two days to die also when they shot him at Skerries on 30 July. Griffith died of apoplexy on 12 August. The Republicans killed Michael Collins on 22 August in an ambush in West Cork in a place whose Irish name means the Mouth of Flowers. Erskine Childers was shot by a Government firing-squad on 24 November. On 7 December the Republicans shot at two pro-Treaty deputies, and killed one of them, Seán Hales. The Government had Rory O'Connor, Liam Mellows, Dick Barrett and Joe McKelvey shot as a reprisal the following day. Liam Lynch, who had given the order under which Hales died, was killed in a fight with Government troops on 10 April 1923. Seventy-seven prisoners in Government hands were shot all told as reprisals for Republican killings, attempted killings and burnings. As many as 12,000 are said to have been imprisoned. Cosgrave, who had taken over the leadership of government of what was now the Irish Free State, was implacable. He reserved his most savage scorn for liberals who ventured to question the humanity of his policy. But it was Kevin O'Higgins, brutally resolute in public though sometimes inclined to clemency in private, who was assassinated, on 10 July 1927. By then the Civil War had been officially over for four years, at a cost of 600 or 700 dead. The violence called into being by the great powers in August 1914 had spawned its offspring in Ireland, to end, at least for a time, by its votaries devouring one another.

There succeeded a bitter ice which froze Irish politics for the succeeding generations. It was an ice that burned those caught in it. The adversaries remained hopelessly trapped within it from the Treaty debates whose bloody successor made for a permanent justification of the violence perpetrated by each side, and the arctic hatred with which they confronted one another asserted the sanctity above politics of the means by which they had elected to settle their accounts. Both sides made great play with their titles to foundation of the new Ireland with such further devolution as they could obtain for it; both sides ignored their evidence of their own emotional deference to that British militarism which had called them into political being in the first place. Neither Griffith nor de Valera was intended by Nature to resort to violence; Griffith for long formally opposed it, de Valera nominally supported it but constantly sought within its cult to keep it limited, defensive, and if possible inoperative. Both men extolled the legacies of violent revolutionaries, Griffith with patient editorial science, de Valera in romantic terms. Both were intellectually defenceless when their academic conservation of the past was forced by Collins to show itself consistent with the present. In their hearts neither was at ease in Collins's world, although both found his charm even harder to resist than his logic. But Griffith's biggest guns were always words on paper, while de Valera to the very eve of the Civil War was still talking about pikes as though anything more modern were a social solecism. Griffith had worked out his ideology, and if he had to pretend the new Sinn Féin, so different from the old, was the correct realization of it, he could always hope to edge it back towards his original conception. De Valera had no such solace. He had inherited something; he had become something; and now he was nothing once more, worse than nothing, reviled and hunted by men to whom but yesterday he had been the symbol of their identity. He had been the hero of the Rising he did not want; now he had to be the villain of the Civil War he did not want—that or some sort of mascot whose custodians seemed to forget its existence.

The Civil War was his Gethsemane, and when he rose again there would be many to call him Messiah, and others to call him Judas. In fact, the figure in the Passion whom he most acutely resembled at this point was Pontius Pilate. But Gethsemane was there for Pontius Pilate nonetheless.

In March 1922 he had stated repeatedly that the Volunteers would have to 'wade through Irish blood' if the Treaty were ratified. It was denounced as incitement; in a sense it was. But it was also prophecy. Anti-Treaty leaders with no loyalty to him would ensure such a result. So would pro-Treaty leaders when they sought to enforce the Treaty and disarm those who refused consent to their authority. He asserted that those who accused him of fomenting civil war were themselves more liable to cause it by their accusations. He was Jeremiah. He was Jonah. Above all, he was Pilate.

Collins had made a desperate attempt to patch up an electoral agreement with him, to the horror of Griffith and the British. But Collins could not, perhaps would not, hold to it. The country's vote against de Valera in June 1922 was thus a vote he could believe to have obtained by false pretences, in the so-called 'pact election'.

And the war came.

He had little to do with its immediate outbreak, which was caused by Rory O'Connor's seizure of the Four Courts and the ultimate Government action in dislodging him by artillery. He was with Brugha up to hours before the end when they were surrounded in a Dublin hotel: de Valera was got out in time. As the war continued, he made pathetic efforts to play the part he had never wanted by constituting a new government and cabinet. It only reaffirmed his impotence. He was in the wrong war, in the wrong place, in the wrong time. He had constantly worked in Ireland for the politics of coalition within the cult of the Republic: now his place as the accepted President of his people was gone for ever. There might have been many Irish in the past who disputed his title to lead them: he could afford to rest content with his majorities, tailoring his dreams about island unity to suit his rejoicing in acceptance. No such illusions seemed open to him now; and what illusions remained crumbled day by day.

He would never again be more than leader of a faction, but it was, ironically, Cosgrave who made it possible for him to find a new existence, Cosgrave who would have shot him if he had fallen into his hands during the Civil War itself. Cosgrave's services to de Valera were twofold. He was in many ways a far harder man than de Valera. He showed courage and strength in his rule, and it was his leadership rather than the will of his admittedly talented subordinates (de Valera had not had anything like the best of the political split in terms of the intellect of his following). But having come to power in the baptism of fire of the Civil War, Cosgrave never grew out of the idea of government by repression. As he moved more and more into actions which inevitably soured much initially favourable opinion against him, he invited constitutional opposition to profit by his severity. His actions, in insisting in 1927 that any political party which sought nomination must be ready to take the Treaty oath, forced de Valera along a firm path which his normal caution and his scattered hostages to fortune might otherwise have prevented his taking.

Cosgrave again opened the future for de Valera by his positive achievements in government, on which a wise successor must build. Here again he gave de Valera a sense of direction. Cosgrave ruled, not reigned. He enabled de Valera to reign again, by so clearly opening up the lines of rule.

He began his services to de Valera by imprisoning him. The Civil War by

then was in fact over, partly by de Valera's officially asking the
Republicans to lay down their arms, partly by the Republicans of
themselves deciding that the struggle was impossible. Cosgrave had
reimposed order, but at a cost to himself which would ultimately
overthrow his government. A General Election was to take place in August
1923. De Valera was arrested campaigning in Clare at Ennis on 15 August
and held without trial in various gaols until 16 July 1924. He had been
triumphantly re-elected for Clare and returned to Ennis for a meeting on
the anniversary of his arrest:

> I am afraid I would disappoint a number here if I were not to start by saying,
> 'Well as I was saying to you when we were interrupted' . . .[1]

The Government's agreement that the Boundary Commission should be
shelved and the *status quo* confirmed gave de Valera all the pleasures of
Cassandra without the preliminary rape. He was asked to co-operate with
the Labour Party, which was uneasily fulfilling the role of Parliamentary
opposition on national even more than on labour questions and yearned
for him to take over its work. But he virtuously declined to take the oath,
even though since December 1922 Labour had been acting under an
admirably dignified rubric which condemned forcing the oath and good-
naturedly pledged allegiance to George V and any other head of state
throughout the world who might deserve it. As to Ulster on 10 December
1925 he declared:

> It is hard to be calm when one remembers that it is our fairest province that is
> being cut off. The Ulster that the Irishman of every province loves best next
> to his own. The Ulster of Cuchulain, the Ulster of the Red Branch Knights.
> The Ulster of the O'Neills and the O'Donnells. The Ulster of Benburb and
> the Yellow Ford. The Ulster in whose sacred sod rest the bones of Patrick,
> Columcille and Brian of the Tributes.[2]

If he had come straight out and said that he had no more to contribute on
the subject of Northern Ireland than Cosgrave, he could hardly have been
more explicit. To the ugly logic of the *apartheid* sub-state being left to its
Unionist leaders' dubious devices by London and Dublin alike he offered a
mish-mash of mythology, hagiography, genealogy and Tudor and Stuart
history, to say nothing of a sentence whose syntax, if it meant anything,
implied that no Irishmen existed in Ulster. On the other hand, he is said on
fair authority to have intervened against assassination attempts on
MacNeill, O'Higgins and his wife's old admirer, now Minister for Finance,

Ernest Blythe. When O'Higgins was in fact killed two years later de Valera was absolutely unequivocal:

> The assassination of Mr O'Higgins is murder and is inexcusable from any standpoint. . . .
> It is a crime that cuts at the root of representative government, and no one who realizes what the crime means can do otherwise than deplore and condemn it.
> Every right-minded individual will deeply sympathize with the bereaved widow in her agony.[3]

Meanwhile on 11 March 1926 de Valera had resigned from the Presidency of Sinn Féin, on the issue of entering the Free State Dáil once the oath had been removed. A majority was against his wish so to do, and he ended a term of office commenced in 1917.[4] The IRA had cut itself off from Sinn Féin the previous November. According to de Valera himself, he had decided to quit public life and confided his intention to a young Dublin lieutenant of his, Seán Lemass, who had made the initial running with Countess Markiewicz on his proposal. Both men were becoming impatient with its visionaries and it was not with a hope of retirement that they were becoming impatient—Lemass was wise to be sceptical about de Valera's intentions of retirement, and had some 33 years ahead in which to make the most of his scepticism. Lemass was pre-eminently the man for the political nuts and bolts, and by 17 April he was ready to present de Valera with the raw basis of a new political party from his supporters in the Sinn Féin minority. It was decided to call it 'Fianna Fáil (the Republican party)', the first term, meaning 'Warriors of Ireland' (a Gaelic name for the Irish Volunteers) being a genuflection to de Valera's pieties; the second, claiming the inheritance of anti-Treaty sentiment, a concession to Lemass's realism. Significantly it was the first name which won celebrity: Lemass's realism had some time to wait before it could reach symbolic acceptance. For all that, the work in building up the party was Lemass's. De Valera was back in America in March and April 1927, again from December 1927 to February 1928, and once again from November 1929 for six months. He once more had success to show his mother: and with Uncle Charlie's death he could now demand her undisputed prime attention, the Redemptorists having the person of his brother. She died on 12 June 1932 leaving as her final irony her house to them jointly. But he had made her the mother of a President once more, in the previous March.

In forming Fianna Fáil, de Valera had appealed to pragmatists, but his psychological fulfilment obtained its meed of matriarchal figures—Mrs

Pearse, Mrs Clarke, and, less matriarchal but more vociferous, Countess
Markiewicz. Mary MacSwiney, Hanna Sheehy-Skeffington, and others
remained in Sinn Féin. IRA leaders isolated from their Army by its
disengagement from Sinn Féin followed him, notably Liam Lynch's
successor, Frank Aiken. He had a hard nucleus of Easter Rising youthful
veterans around himself: his exact contemporary, Seán T. Ó Ceallaigh, Dr
James Ryan, Lemass and MacEntee, the first three having served in 1916 in
the General Post Office, the last in co. Louth. Cumann na nGaedheal, the
Government party, with the Speaker, was reduced to 47 deputies, in the
General Election of June 1927, while Fianna Fáil faced the Dáil with 45.
The critical question of the oath in the Civil War looked liked forcing an
abstentionist policy on them. But the country was far less concerned about
the oath than was de Valera; it wanted a viable alternative to Cosgrave, and
it apparently trusted him to make himself one. De Valera ultimately
converted the missing formula from a problem to its solution and
proclaimed the taking of the oath an 'empty formula', once Cosgrave
declared that candidates had to take it. De Valera was accused of having
caused one Civil War by refusing to take the oath; he replied that he had
prevented a second by taking it. 'It is never easy to pass under the yoke', he
acknowledged grimly. He had his revenge in almost turning the
Government out on his first day. A new election in September increased the
totals of both major parties to 67 for Cosgrave and 57 for de Valera, gains
at the expense of the smaller parties. But de Valera chose both to
rationalize his own past, and to milk future support from present
intransigents, by refusing to acknowledge the legislature's legitimacy, even
though he supplied it with a vigorous Opposition. Lemass showed his
pragmatism in a somewhat chilling way by referring in March 1928 to
Fianna Fáil as 'a slightly constitutional party': the implication remained
that constitutional means would be employed only so far as they yielded
results. It is doubtful if de Valera really believed this sort of thing any more.
Lemass, whose brother had been done to death by Government forces in
the Dublin mountains during the Civil War, and who was not yet thirty,
was of a generation which had come of age in war; war was only an
aberration in de Valera's life. Had he been forced to take the oath with full
panoply, instead of in a hole-and-corner fashion in which he was enabled
pointedly to set aside the Bible from the process, he had apparently
determined to refuse and devote himself to the revival of the Irish
language.

In the event the Government, strong in achievement but weak in
propaganda, supplied the Opposition with its issues. Fianna Fáil might

appear archaic at first glance in the face of McGilligan's Shannon hydro-electric achievement or Patrick Hogan's agricultural reforms. But Ernest Blythe's shilling off the miserly old age pension offered a useful target. As Professor John A. Murphy has stressed, the Government came to look like a custodian of the propertied interests, impressive as its team was. De Valera's was a much more popular party, with a far more sophisticated organization on the parish level. It seemed to many to speak with a Left-wing voice: in fact it was a populist voice, summed up when the change of government in 1932 was styled 'the flight from the top hat'. But even the political behaviour involved here was in itself an old song: de Valera was using much the same crusade as that which Sinn Féin had employed underneath its patriotic rhetoric in 1917, charging opponents with having grown too gentlemanly for their roots and constituents. Parnell's party had popularized itself by similar appeal in the 1880s. As for the Left-wing image, it was a classic illustration of Marx's argument about the bourgeoisie's readiness to enlist the proletariat as allies when necessary, and discard them subsequently. Fianna Fáil took exactly as much of the rhetoric and programmes of the Left as it needed to give itself an appearance of radicalism and a lien on the loyalties of revolutionaries, social and national. Cosgrave under threat fell into the blunder of playing the politics of 'red scare' in his last years of office. He tried it on the wrong man. For all of Cosgrave's strength, he grew obsessed by de Valera: when de Valera turned in his direction Cosgrave gave a fine zoological exhibition of a rodent fascinated by a reptile. Hence in the winter of 1931–32 he saw means of stirring up the Catholic clergy who were proving depressingly Christian in the forgiveness many of them were extending to the unrepentant prodigal son, despite their having excommunicated him for opposing lawful government in the Civil War. As with Redmond, so with Cosgrave: the priests disliked their support being taken for granted. A 'Red Scare' might reawaken their alarm and stampede their flocks back to the government. But the thing was self-contradictory from the outset. The concept adumbrated by Cosgrave's more ideological anti-Communist allies, such as the Police Commissioner and admirer of Mussolini, General Eoin O'Duffy, was that the Republican movement outside Fianna Fáil was going Communist under the auspices of figures like Peadar O'Donnell, and would seize the means of enslaving the country to Moscow once de Valera had come to power. The hypothesis, however, cast de Valera for Kerensky; and there was no way in which Cosgrave could convince himself or anyone else that he saw de Valera as a Kerensky. And de Valera, having seen one Red Scare rise and fall in the United States, knew exactly how to address the issue: show dignity, say little, and wait. Fianna Fáil had some success in turning the same trick, but in a somewhat less European context. In place of the Government's eye to precautions in Italy, premonitions in Spain and proselytism in Russia, they paraded fears as to Ireland's enslavement to the interests, financial and social, which had held her in thrall for 700 years. Cosgrave, it was argued, was being kept in power by a combination of crypto-Unionists and Freemasons. Northern Ireland existed as a horrid warning: the Orange hegemony there was Masonic (actually only quasi-Masonic as was also true of the Knights of St Columbanus and many influential Catholic organizations in the Irish Free State), and it was also, of course, Unionist. Sophisticated Fianna Fáil theory, the brighter for a little Marxist sprinkling with no danger of a deluge, noted that financial interests flourishing under the Union would wish to perpetuate their hold on Irish productivity, and hence Cosgrave's interests must be those of the former holders of power. Unsophisticated Fianna Fáil theory assumed that those of their number who failed to get jobs were done down by Masonic conspiracy: they could, after all, hardly be expected to welcome the thought of having suffered discrimination on their own lack of merit.

Although hostility to the Freemasons was not new, and the Masonic record did involve some flagrant cases of preferential advancement, it was the new world-wide depression which made the search for scapegoats much more urgent. And just to keep the pot boiling the Holy Ghosts in Blackrock, former patrons, teachers and employers of de Valera, were producing their own evidence that the Masons were behind the Russian Revolution. Among other supporters of this thesis was the Very Revd John Charles McQuaid, CSSp, Superior of Blackrock College, whom de Valera's influence or at least obvious favour would later make Archbishop of Dublin. If Cosgrave thought he had a monopoly on bogies he was to find himself sadly mistaken.

De Valera triumphed in the March 1932 elections. Cosgrave had done his best to prevent 1932 being a revolution. How far did de Valera make it one? He was by nature a consensus politician, preferring that he presided over the consensus, but capable of manipulating, and even acceding to, consensus when in Opposition. Hence he was unsympathetic to ideas among Republicans in and out of Fianna Fáil that the civil service, the judiciary, the army and the police be politicized. He removed certain high-ranking police officers, notably O'Duffy, and Collins's spy in Dublin Castle during British rule, David Neligan. He kept a wary eye on the army. He insisted on an austerity and apparent self-abnegation in the civil service, more or less maintaining principles of anonymity outside of official duties: officially the pattern was British, and he had little desire here to emulate the 'spoils' system of the USA, but in practice the style of life and control suggested something more akin to Roman Catholic religious orders. He put in his men when vacancies occurred in the judiciary, and having much fewer lawyers among his ranks than were possessed by his opponents, he made some choices from allies—or associates—as well as from the party faithful; George Gavan Duffy, for instance, had been one of the delegates who had signed the Treaty and entered the Free State Dáil, but whose liberalism over executions of Republicans quickly earned him the hatred of Cosgrave. He found Government jobs for a few persons whose abilities and loyalties had won special favour from him. He used a compulsory Irish admission test as a means of compelling at least symbolic deference to his national ideals and thus helped insure against a civil service continuum of Vicars of Bray.

His leadership had to deal with the problem that his notions of the authority of the father of his country, spiritual or otherwise, had been formed in the deferential era before the First World War and there was little in his make-up which sympathized with the liberalism of the 1920s. It was not only that he and his men, like Cosgrave and his men, were alarmed by the flood of what they saw as morally destructive literature, newspapers, films and other forms of communications, and that the protection of the state from invasions by such cultural barbarism was as natural to him as to his predecessors; for all of his place on the far edges of the Irish Renaissance through association particularly with Sinéad, and MacDonagh, and more vaguely through his inspiration in the 1920s to young writers like Seán Ó Faoláin and Frank O'Connor (Michael O'Donovan), he symbolized that style of the Irish Revolution which had revolted against the Irish Renaissance. He thought of *Knocknagow* when he thought of the culture of the new Ireland; his administration beheld with tranquillity the Censorship Board's banning of Ó Faoláin's novel *Bird Alone* in 1936, or of *The Green Lion* by Francis Hackett who had done so much to sway the *New Republic* to his cause, came to live in Ireland, and now in disgust moved to the somewhat less restrictive climate of Denmark. De Valera of course did not introduce censorship; the Board was established in 1930. He simply reaped the rewards of liberal annoyance about it, and quietly accorded with it. The same would be true with respect to other Cosgrave incursions on civil liberties, such as the outlawry of divorce which so infuriated Yeats.

His regime also went through a parade of abrogating ties with the British state which his predecessors were condemned for having permitted, but the process was in fact a further instance of continuity. He had taken his stand with perfect poise on the stepping-stones vacated by Cosgrave; he merely invited his audience to contemplate the far-off hills while allowing him to place their feet. In general, his performance was one of shrewd exploitation of the ignorance of the new British politicians: already his longevity was beginning to tell against his adversaries. His old tactic of opposing partition in order grudgingly to sweep up the concessions proffered to offset its maintenance worked well towards the end of the decade. The triumph of 1938 is admirably placed in perspective by Professor Murphy:

> The Anglo-Irish agreements of 1938 were popularly regarded as a triumph for de Valera and characteristically exploited for election purposes by Fianna Fáil. The return of the British-held naval bases was the *pièce de résistance* of these agreements though it may have been less a matter of 'Dev getting back the ports' than a British decision that they weren't worth the bother and risk of holding on to them. At any rate, the scene was set for the Irish decision to remain neutral, though the chances of success of such a policy were slim.[5]

It must be stressed that for all of de Valera's perennial stress on the vitality of state sovereignty—or, in the words of Pearse, 'the sovereign people'—there was nothing visionary about this achievement. Neville Chamberlain, argues A.J.P. Taylor, saw the gesture of the ports as a first exercise in appeasement; but de Valera intended it as the insurance for independence in time of war. If he had since 1919 looked more closely at the American Revolutionary settlement he realized that in the aftermath of that also there was a period of almost a dozen years before the British would evacuate critical installations and that American security was so much bound up with the gain that self-indulgent symbols of chauvinism were firmly sacrificed to it.

De Valera spoke in terms of longstanding commitment; he behaved in terms of longstanding policy. Between sovereignty *de jure* (involving Northern Ireland) and sovereignty *de facto* (involving the 26 counties) it was the latter he worked for, the former he talked about. But he was exceedingly alert—it was one of the benefits of his parochialism—to the way in which apparently remote developments could be squeezed to his advantage. The amours of Edward VIII, for instance, became de Valera's means of implementing External Association; if Baldwin wished him to co-operate in the dropping of the King, then Baldwin would have to accept the way in which he would acknowledge the next one. He played a smooth hand in response to Baldwin's formal inquiry whether Mrs Wallis Simpson should be recognized as Queen, or the King should abdicate, or Mrs Simpson should not become Queen but the King, having married her, should not abdicate: he chose the unusual course of favouring the third, pointing out that he did so 'on the assumption that divorce was a recognized institution in England'. It was an admirable way of indicating that the social and cultural differences between the islands had now been extended to the recognition of divergent majority custom in divergent legislated moral codes. Thanks to Cosgrave's moral protectionism, which he had inherited and implemented, his moment of demure glory had arrived: England's difficulty was Ireland's opportunity. Naturally his advice carried with it the unspoken corollary that what would do for divorce-ridden 'England' would not, of course, do for monogamous Ireland, and Baldwin himself had shown the inapplicability of the King to Ireland. De Valera then declined to call the legislature for a week after Edward VIII's actual abdication, thus creating a crisis in which Edward might still be considered King in Ireland. Hence during that week, the Irish Free State was an independent monarchy. The Puckish humour involved in the use of prolonging the reign of Edward VIII for the purpose of taking a great leap forward towards full independence was characteristic of the private natures of both de Valera and his chief prompter in the matter, Seán MacEntee.

Bills were then rushed through the Dáil eliminating the King and the Governor-General from the Free State Constitution, and recognizing that so long as the 'following nations, that is to say, Australia, Canada, Great Britain, New Zealand and South Africa' (de Valera would be delighted to demonstrate the radicalism of alphabetical order), were associated with the Free State and the King continued to act on their behalf for the appointment of diplomatic and consular representatives and the conclusion of international agreements, 'the King so recognized may, and is hereby authorized to, act on behalf of Saorstát Éireann for the like purposes, as and when advised by the Executive Council so to do'. It was a magnificent reminder of the common origin between de Valera and George Bernard Shaw in his capacity as author of *The Apple Cart*. It was also a reminder that when considerations of extending his power in the state he administered were involved, he would sacrifice yet another link with Ulster Unionist Protestantism without the slightest hesitation.[6]

The Free State Constitution had been given under a British Act of Parliament and owed much to intellectuals like Lionel Curtis and Darrell Figgis, and while a fine secular constitution, redolent with guarantees of personal and civil liberties which might well be the envy of any European liberal, Cosgrave had brutally amended it. In practice, British rule in Ireland had given the Irish representative democracy, but had been much less ready to extend the British tradition of civil liberties. Cosgrave had eliminated the referendum and initiative, and brought in codes of repression including the use of military tribunals with provision for increasing the penalties accorded by law to specific crimes and without provision for appeal. The rags of popular militarism still produced many crimes of violence, and Cosgrave had been determined to stamp them out. De Valera removed the Oath of Allegiance from the Constitution, the Governor-General's discretionary functions and the right of judicial appeal to the Privy Council, before finessing the King. In 1936 he also abolished the Free State Senate, which had been a bastion of minority (and plutocratic) interests. He offset this by a cultivation of the Unionist institution, Trinity College, Dublin, nominally with respect to its dissident contributions to Irish nationalism, actually to show the world how well he treated Protestants: they were to have patronage without power.

The weakness of the secular acceptability of the Free State Constitution lay in its having derived from the Westminster Parliament. But de Valera was not prepared to follow the American secular example by claiming that the Irish people gave themselves the new Constitution, *tout court*. He did use the US Constitution formula 'We the people' and with alterations followed American precedent in the preamble with the words

> seeking to promote the common good, with due observance of Prudence, Justice and Charity, so that the dignity and freedom of the individual may be assured, true social order attained, the unity of the country restored, and concord established with other nations.
>
> Do hereby adopt, enact and give to ourselves this Constitution.

He even reworked the American aim of 'a more perfect Union' to drag partition into it; the Constitution was to restore 'the unity of our country'. The preamble began, however

> In the Name of the Most Holy Trinity, from Whom is all authority and to Whom, as our final end, all actions of men and States must be referred,

and informed 'We the people' that before they adopted, enacted and gave to themselves this constitution they began by

> Humbly acknowledging all our obligations to our Divine Lord, Jesus Christ, Who sustained our fathers through centuries of trial,
>
> Gratefully remembering their heroic and unremitting struggle to regain the rightful independence of our Nation,

and then did their bit for the common good, Prudence, Justice and Charity intervening.

The Irish Constitution of 1937 itself went so far in legislating current Roman Catholic social thought on education, private property, the family and principles of social policy in general that the future Professor Michael Oakeshott placed extracts from it in his section of 'Catholicism' in *The Social and Political Doctrines of Contemporary Europe* in 1939, thus distinguishing it from Representative Democracy, Communism, Fascism and National Socialism, to which the rest of his book devoted itself. But it was Article 44 which clinched the matter, and in so doing absolutely divided the country between Northern Ireland with its Protestant majority and the remnant.

> 1. 1°. The State acknowledges that the homage of public worship is due to Almighty God. It shall hold His Name in reverence, and shall respect and honour religion.

In theory, of course, Northern Ireland could not object to that. It may have given de Valera a vicious satisfaction that it could hardly acknowledge its objection in practice or, as he would say, *de facto*. But—

> 2°. The State recognizes the special position of the Holy Catholic Apostolic and Roman Church as the guardian of the Faith professed by the great majority of the citizens.
>
> 3°. The State also recognizes the Church of Ireland, the Presbyterian Church of Ireland, the Methodist Church in Ireland, the Religious Society of Friends in Ireland, as well as the Jewish Congregations and the other religious denominations existing in Ireland at the date of the coming into operation of this Constitution.

Northern Ireland must see that as wholly unacceptable, not that it would have been looking for acceptable material. It beheld with anger the grandiose assumptions of Article 2, claiming the whole island, modified by the realistic Article 3, 'pending the reunification of the national territory' for which time limiting the Constitution's operation to the 26 counties. But it did not appreciate that the recognition of the special position of the Catholic Church was a tacit abandonment of serious claims on 'our lost six counties'. Henceforth the six counties were but a rhetorical and diplomatic device as far as de Valera was concerned.

The Constitution, therefore, took de Valera off the hook of serious activity for reintegration and did so under the most unquestionable of auspices. It also ensured that de Valera had a free hand in many of the areas he wanted it, such as international relations. With the Holy Trinity behind him and the special position (whatever that might be) of the Roman Catholic Church before him, he could snap his fingers at Bishops who wanted him to back Franco, outlaw Communists, smile at Mussolini or quarantine the USSR. Fascism was not a threat in Ireland—a ridiculous 'Blueshirt' movement under O'Duffy fizzled ingloriously out to the discomfiture of Opposition leaders foolish enough to have backed it without Fascist intent on their parts—but a Christian Front on the lines of the CEDA in Spain or Dollfuss's movement in Austria might have been. De Valera had taken the Catholic high ground. It also meant that the State was redrawn with as little alteration as possible in its general administrative lines; de Valera could afford to squelch later more radical proposals about vocational reorganization. Catholicism never had fully accepted representative democracy, and in a world of upheaval its more intellectual votaries might be tempted to flirt with systems more in keeping with Vatican social dogma. De Valera had found the means of containing Catholic rhetoric while keeping a tradition of representative democracy.

There was also a social aspect to the undefined 'special position' of Catholicism. It was an acknowledgement of the former outlaw status of the religion in the eighteenth century, and the constitutional affirmation of the principles of its architecture in the nineteenth: that the Catholic church in any village must be built so as to overawe the Protestant church. It was the assertion that the under-class, the despised caste, were the masters now. In this sense, it was not clericalist so much as populist. The same thing had applied to some of de Valera's own intervention in church-state controversies. He might seem to take an official Catholic position; he was in fact usually taking one reflecting popular Catholic attitudes. In 1931, still in Opposition, he had championed Catholic clerical criticism of the appointment of a Protestant County Librarian in Mayo, but he had done so on the basis of what the people wanted and how little a Trinity College product might know how best to meet their cultural needs.

The Constitution is sometimes seen as deference towards the Catholic hierarchy and clergy many of whom still darkly recalled the former excommunication of the President, or Taoiseach as he was now to be called (a Gaelicization of the term 'Chief' personally applied to de Valera, as to Parnell, by his followers). It was not. De Valera's own former leanings to the spiritual priesthood now received their fulfilment. He was legislating not as a son of the Church, but as one of its fathers, albeit without actual ordination. The point is of importance. If we imagine that de Valera was earnestly trimming his sails to make the most of clerical wind, we miss the point. This was not an attempt to conciliate the Church. It was an adoption, enactment and giving to himself of an instrument which affirmed that he was the Church. It is not even Caesaro-papalism. He repudiated comparisons with the Napoleonic concordat, although it contained useful precedents which he employed. But he was no Napoleon or Charlemagne or Barbarossa seeking to use the Church for his interests. He saw no distinction between its true interests and his. Professor Murphy remarks that it 'is not easy to see where and why Éamon de Valera drew the line between Christ and Caesar'[7]: he did not draw it at all. His psyche had never sought to answer his rejection by his mother in resentment, but in fulfilment, and there would be peace in the house left by Mrs Wheelwright to her two sons. He did not claim to be a better son than the other; he had sought always to make the other his friend. Their interests must be one. Only thus could Mother be reassured that all was well. He had not been driven forth by her, he must always assure himself, whatever the realities; sometimes his way took him where she was not. But he would always return, and always be welcome, as welcome as—but not more welcome than—the other son, his brother, really distinct and equal but inseparable in spirit if not in space. Mother, Éamon, Thomas: Ireland, Taoiseach, Clergy. In the Name of the Most Holy Trinity . . .

The people gave themselves the Constitution by 685,105 votes to 526,945. The abstentions made for a minority in acceptance. But Éamon de Valera had no further use for abstentionism.

The first Papal Nuncio, Monsignor Paschal Robinson, had been appointed in 1929 under the Cosgrave government, whereupon the Fianna Fáil Opposition announced that the Catholic hierarchy had been insulted in not having been consulted on the matter in advance. This was unscrupulous, albeit, for recently excommunicated men, shrewd: and many of them would have felt the Catholic bishops must be given every proof that their real friends were the ardent patriots and not, by implication, the allegedly Freemason-allied Government. This sort of thing made for a competition between the parties for individual episcopal regard, and 'individual' was the right word. It was an old joke that Papal diplomats assigned to Ireland complained about the difficulty of dealing with twenty-eight popes. De Valera's Constitution was, in part, intended to undercut this situation by putting the twenty-eight, their subordinates and their flocks within a form of government, not Erastian but no longer independent. His Constitution made no official claims on the Bishops, although it assigned them official status: but their freedom had been invisibly circumscribed. It may have been the case that he wanted his more anti-clerical immediate followers to believe that he was making concessions to their feeling: not all of them had outgrown that sense of disillusion with Catholicism resulting from excommunication, while among their former Republican comrades, as with their Fenian forbears, many had not returned to the Church at all. De Valera's Jewish follower, Robert Briscoe, in one of the many hilarious stories in his *For the Life of Me,* tells of the problems of organizers of the newly-born Fianna Fáil in 1927 having to deal with the intransigence of its Republicans on Mass attendance. Making allowance for Judaism as well as for apostasy proved almost too much for one local boss:

> They all went into Mass, while I remained with the car from which we would speak when it was over. O'Leary turned back and said to me, 'Will you not go in to Mass?'
>
> 'I don't go to Mass', I replied.
>
> 'Everybody goes to Mass here [Ballyseedy, co. Kerry], you'll have to do likewise.'
>
> I began to explain the difference in our faiths, when O'Leary interrupted me. Speaking between clenched teeth he said, 'Haven't we enough bloody trouble explaining Fianna Fáil without having to explain you as well? At least go to the door and *pretend* you're going to Mass!'
>
> I complied.[8]

But while Fianna Fáil votaries recognized the necessity to 'bow the knee' it was for few of its founders a matter of the cheerful ecumenism of Briscoe; it had been their Church, not his, and it had outlawed them. It is easier to forgive a prodigal son than a prodigal Church. De Valera, with his experience of forgiving and suppressing his injuries at the hands of a prodigal parent, had no difficulty in making the transition: unlike some of his followers he easily distinguished between pronouncements of individual and even collective bishops, and his own possession of Catholicism. As he saw it, the bishops who condemned him had exceeded their pastoral remit. In his fatherly fashion, he had now given his people a Constitution (to give themselves) which would protect the bishops against their own possible theological backsliding. He would save the clergy, as he would save the laity, from themselves.

After the Constitution had been adopted, the Bishops began to discover their weakness. Pressure for vocational organization had already been mounting. As Professor Joseph Lee points out in an essay of profound thought and vast entertainment on the episode, the advocates believed that:

> In the vocational order occupational groups would elect self-governing corporations, which would co-operate closely together to wield effective

social and economic power throughout society. Corporatism would curb class conflict and counter the growing threat to individual liberty from state bureaucracy.[9]

They took their stand on the encyclical of Pope Pius XI issued in 1931, *Quadragesimo Anno*. De Valera's smashing electoral victory of June 1938 was followed by his appointment of a Commission on Vocational Organization in 1939, headed by Michael John Browne, the Catholic Bishop of Galway. It consisted of twenty-five enthusiastic, heterogeneous and voluble public persons, and its 'composition . . . suggests a conviction on Mr de Valera's part that all viewpoints should be heard at as interminable and irascible a length as possible'. Its 300,000-word report was presented in November 1943 and published in August 1944:

> Fianna Fáil had enjoyed yet another triumph in the general election of May 1944, and Mr de Valera was in no humour to be deprived of the spoils of office by promoting a vocational assembly as a non-Party power centre in Irish life. Except for a few carping and trivial criticisms, the government simply buried the Report.

The Commission, in fact, was less Papal than populist, and while suffering from the obsessions and suspicions of most populist critiques, held it in common with them that it asked questions which conventional politics were avoiding and burying to the detriment of society. But although de Valera himself was a highly populist politician, it was essentially populism filtered through his own perceptions. In the Dáil Treaty debates he said on 6 January 1922:

> . . . I have been brought up amongst the Irish people. I was reared in a labourer's cottage here in Ireland. I have not lived solely amongst the intellectuals. The first fifteen years of my life that formed my character were lived amongst the Irish people down in Limerick; therefore, I know what I am talking about; and whenever I wanted to know what the Irish people wanted I had only to examine my own heart and it told me straight off what the Irish people wanted.[10]

Twenty years after, he was not inclined to look to other guides. However imaginary and self-protective his vision of his rural youth in 1922, it was by 1944—the year after his 'athletic youths and comely maidens' broadcast—almost entirely sealed off from the reality of what he did not want to hear. It did not mean that he had lost his touch: in these very years he was showing himself a masterly diplomat in the struggle for neutrality, and a master-tactician in the winning of elections. But his people were now firmly locked into his heart, and he had no intention of calling them into creative activity from the Paradise into which he had willed them. The Commission envisaged, however naïvely, a role of popular initiative: de Valera only wanted the psychological gratification of popular response. The dictates of his wartime diplomacy in which, with far more rigour than his old inspiration, Woodrow Wilson, he had decreed neutrality in thought, word and deed, demanded of him also, as he saw it, a censorship as rigorous in news and comment as that he had inherited in literature. He himself knew much of what went on in the world; but he allowed his people to know only what was good for them, and this did not include aids to constructive thought on foreign affairs, and hence on domestic affairs. The war ended, the news censorship ended, the principle remained. And with it was the increasing darkening of his sight. He could now see very little. And what he saw most vividly was what he wanted the Irish people to want.

But the episode meant that inevitably idealists were disillusioned and soured: the ice had condemned de Valera's political Opposition to impotence until 1948, and it was now hardening around other would-be constructive critics. Michael John Browne was left to atrophy into a bitter, repressive reactionary; so was another great advocate of vocationalism, the future Bishop of Cork, Cornelius Lucey. Dr John Dignan, the Bishop of Clonfert, produced later in 1944 a 'social benefits scheme which', wrote my father, Professor R. Dudley Edwards, 'was remarkable in its day as being 20 years ahead of current economic thinking'.[11] Just as the only response to the Commission had been hostility from James Ryan, and contempt from Seán Lemass, now Dignan found his proposals rejected with cruel sarcasm by Seán MacEntee. De Valera's own familiar friend, Dr John Charles McQuaid of Dublin, ventured to remonstrate at the utter refusal of the Government to grant concessions to overworked and underpaid teachers, driven to stage a major strike in Dublin in 1946. These were the very people whom de Valera's use of idealism had lit with enthusiasm, only to find themselves trapped in a soul-destroying system mechanically directed by a ruthlessly conservative civil service, and intended to be enforced by corporal punishment. The Archbishop of Dublin was no more fortunate than his fellows: he was spared the public humiliation of Ministerial derision; but all knew that his advice had been scorned by his old patron. The wretched teachers were forced back to work without an additional penny, the schoolchildren were left as best they could to compensate for months of lost education, and the Bishops ate out their hearts in rage and shame.

There was an element of *hubris* in all of this. The Bishops might bury their individual differences and invoke the 'special position' he had given them. But the Constitution was the wand of the sorcerer. Lemass in his blunt, innocent pragmatism had said during its making 'You know, Chief, we can't very well make the Constitution a manifesto of Fianna Fáil policy'.[12] De Valera had known better: in the higher sense it would be. The Constitution of his native country had been conceived 150 years before his own—the anniversary would not have escaped him, few anniversaries did. And his Constitution's provisions had the merit that, flexible in his hand, they would prove perilous in the extreme to any wayward apprentice who might seek to purloin it. He did not, of course, expect to be defeated in February 1948. His normally impeccable timing did not desert him in calling the election; but he reckoned without the action of the ice in shifting his widely diverse opponents into a phalanx of hatred against himself. He had seen Cosgrave's party in Opposition fall and fall. It had been caught hopelessly in its confrontation against the British government over the oath, the refusal to pay land annuities, and the emasculation of the Governor-General. The British had made matters much worse by making it quite clear they assumed in 1932 that de Valera's time in power would be short, and hence their own interests lay in support of Cosgrave. Cosgrave on his side had to deal with split and Opposition competition, with the stampede of his followers into O'Duffy's movement and its subsequent collapse, and finally the problems of regrouping into a new party, Fine Gael, painting itself into a conservative corner. It loyally supported his neutrality during the war, but he got the credit, as he had done for his earlier use of nationalist solidarity to withstand British economic pressure against his reforms in the 1930s. The Labour party, long disenchanted with him, divided itself by an ugly witch-hunt against supposed Reds. But de Valera was vulnerable to a repetition of his own tactics, to a 'slightly constitutional' party, drawing on Republican fervour and profiting from Government conservatism by adroit use of the rhetoric of social justice.

With the war over, a formidable dissident emerged to challenge him. Seán MacBride was the son of Yeats's beloved Maud Gonne and of the courageous Boer War leader John MacBride, who was shot by the British after the Easter Rising (in which he had been second-in-command in Jacob's Biscuit Factory under Thomas MacDonagh). It was as though the gods who had smiled on de Valera's birth as a Republican were deserting him. It was held that the place of the birthright seemed now to be usurped by a mess of pottage; it was also held that it was a very poor quality of pottage. MacBride had parted company with the IRA, but as lawyer won

many plaudits for his defences of several of their number who fell foul of
the Government during the war. He had held some regard for de
Valera—but he now turned his energies in the direction of disposal of his
once 'dear Chief'. His party, Clann na Poblachta, showed early signs of
posing a real challenge to Fianna Fáil, and de Valera's choice of an
election-date in February 1948 was clearly to nip it in the bud. He had
assumed that Fine Gael's stodgy conservatism would leave it cold to
MacBride's excitable quasi-Republicanism and preachment of Ireland in
the dollar area. But the sweets of office, and the pleasure of overthrowing
him, were too strong. In his youth he had been the agent of coalition as the
compromise candidate who could unite Griffith and Count Plunkett,
MacNeill and Brugha. He now saw John A. Costello, an ordinary Fine
Gael member, head a coalition which effected a similar union.

But while his own ageing and largely lack-lustre team were put in the
shade by Costello's, that depended on the volatile MacBride, and
MacBride simply lacked his own ability to hold the conflicting spirits to the
bidding of the sorcerer's wand. It was indeed the 'special position' which
blasted MacBride and his party. The resentful Bishops suddenly coalesced,
in their turn, to demand obeisance to their criticisms of a mild health
scheme for mothers and children. Their grounds were extremely dubious;
those of them whose dioceses lay partly or wholly in Northern Ireland had
been forced to come to terms with the much more sweeping health reforms
of Aneurin Bevan in the British Labour Government. But what really ailed
them was their condemnation by de Valera to a negative aridity, and they
demanded their meed of deference in the only language now left to them.
De Valera had in fact created an alienated clerical intelligentsia, headed by
his own *protégé,* McQuaid. But it was MacBride who was hurled into
political oblivion by the crossfire. The Bishops threw their weight against
MacBride's party colleague, the enthusiastic Dr Noël Browne, who had
won such just celebrity by his campaign against tuberculosis and who now
was fighting for public health on a larger scale. Costello gave way before
the Bishops, and MacBride followed his Taoiseach, deserting his follower.
The wave of protest on behalf of Browne broke over the head of the
Government; Browne and his supporters were returned as independents at
the 1951 election, but MacBride and his party were finished. MacBride did
later win international celebrity: unlike de Valera he was never again to
enjoy it as the counterpart to leadership at home.

A health scheme was clearly needed from the new Fianna Fáil
Government. Again the Bishops became restive, and threatened public
criticism. But de Valera, bringing personal pressure on his old school

friend Cardinal D'Alton of Armagh, outflanked his personal enemies in
the hierarchy by persuading the Bishops to withdraw their hostile press
release from the very jaws of the journalists, pointedly agreed to the
changes in wording of his Government's Bill and restrictions placed on the
legislation, and showed himself the rightful interpreter as well as begetter
of his own Constitution. Archbishop McQuaid was left to dispatch
subsequent morose warnings that 'the fabric of our social life is being
subtly and progressively undermined' and deploring 'the effect on the
educated sections of our society, which such a fear of the unitary or
Socialistic State continues deeply to disturb'.[13] There was a real bitterness
in the reference to the educated sections of society: the Archbishop had not
forgotten de Valera's refusal to help the teachers, and his remark carried
the implication that the de Valera Government was of its nature hostile to
the interests of the educated and likely to deepen their alienation. He was
right, although de Valera's successor, Lemass, was to show an interest in
attracting constructive, if deferential, intellectual support. But McQuaid
himself was reduced to negative impotence in his criticism of de Valera.
The ice had frozen him into a position where he could only justify such
criticism by alleging obviously chimerical dangers of Socialism, and the
alienated intellectuals, however disenchanted by de Valera, would reserve
the major vials of their wrath for Michael John Browne, Cornelius Lucey
and John Charles McQuaid, wholly unaware that they were confronting
victims from their own ranks. De Valera's Constitution had shown itself a
time-bomb in the ice.

With his sense of his own possession of true Irish Catholicism he gave a
signal expression of his superiority in ethics to his episcopal enemies before
his retirement. A very ugly boycott broke out in Fethard-on-Sea, county
Wexford, against the local Protestants, for alleged and unproven support
of a Protestant mother who had departed taking her children from her
Catholic husband. Michael John Browne defended the boycott. De Valera
in the Dáil, speaking as Taoiseach—after the second Costello coalition he
had been re-elected in March 1957 for the last time—condemned it:

> I cannot say that I know every fact, but if, as head of the government, I must
> speak, I can only say, from what has appeared in public, that I regard this
> boycott as ill-conceived, ill-considered and futile for the achievement of the
> purpose for which it seems to have been intended; that I regard it as unjust
> and cruel to confound the innocent with the guilty; that I repudiate any
> suggestion that this boycott is typical of the attitude or conduct of our
> people; that I am convinced that 90 per cent of them look on this matter as I
> do; and that I beg of all who have regard for the fair name, good repute and

spiritual well-being of our nation to use their influence to bring this deplorable affair to a speedy end.[14]

The date was the Fourth of July, 1957. It was American Independence day. But it is worth noticing that, once again, de Valera had no intention of proclaiming his independence of the Church: he was, as usual, speaking for it. He was also speaking for the people of Ireland. Michael John Browne was wrong. So were the Catholics of Fethard-on-Sea. They had shown themselves wanting in his specifications for true Irish Catholicism.

It is important to stress that this was a highly theological pronouncement. De Valera might expect some electoral advantage for his party among liberal intellectuals; he might also expect some alienation of support from pious Galway or Wexford Catholics. This was the father of his people saying what they ought to be in secular and spiritual matters: the term 'spiritual well-being' is highly revelatory of his own 'special position' to the Catholic Church in Ireland. Characteristically, he held to his form of populism by telling the people what they ought to be by asserting this is what they actually were. And, for all of his archaism, it is fine.

And in his darkness he could see the smiles of support from the athletic youths and comely maidens.

> 'Traditional' Ireland had found its noblest personification in Éamon de Valera, whose capacity for heroic self-deception concerning social realities verged on genius.

The writer is Professor Joseph Lee, in the concluding essay to *Ireland 1945–70* which he edited:

> This society, however distorted its self-image, could nevertheless inspire great dedication in the service of its spiritual ideals, sacred or secular, among those unconscious of its materialistic basis. Mr de Valera's Constitution of 1937 ironically codified the 'traditional' values at a moment when post-famine society could be seen to be already doomed by its own innate sterility. It would be melodramatic to claim that 'traditional' Ireland is dead and gone, with de Valera in the grave, though the arcadian Ireland of his dreams would now be buried for ever, had it ever existed. The façade of de Valera's Ireland was already crumbling before his departure because the foundations were rotting. Only the majesty of the man himself concealed some of the worst fissures in the edifice.[15]

In particular, Professor Lee points to the place of emigration from post-war Ireland.

> 'Traditional' Ireland relied for its survival on a human haemorrhage. The prevailing marriage, money and morality nexus depended on it. . . . More

than 500,000 people abandoned their 'traditional' Ireland between 1945 and 1961 as the wave of emigration surged forward.

Dublin Opinion, the pluckily bourgeois monthly humorous journal, fighting to keep a public laughing wryly at the cavernous cracks opening in the ice between ideal and reality, once in the 1950s gave its front-page cartoon to a map of Ireland surmounted by a notice of sale announcing 'OWNERS GOING ABROAD'. The Fethard-on-Sea boycott was in reality a nasty reminder of the obverse of his legend of glorious struggle, but it was, like de Valera himself, a symbol of an era almost done. Social concern about the marriages of others had been a theme in Irish society from Bruree in 1885 to Fethard in 1957; but henceforward society would be fragmented into individuals' anxieties about their own. It also meant the passing of community in a benevolent as well as a censorious form: the new liberalism also meant the new selfishness. De Valera's example of austerity in personal life offers an awesome contrast to that of his party's next generation, notably Mr Charles J. Haughey and his associates, who came into their own under Lemass. His was not a sanctimonious example, although it invited hypocrisy from ambitious underlings anxious to curry favour. He enjoyed revealing it, especially for British acquaintances, taking a childlike pleasure in surprising them into recognition of the charm of his archaism, or, as he would see it, the virtue of his Arcadia.

How did he govern his 'traditional' Ireland? Here his own pre-occupation with being a 'politician by accident' was translated into an entire scheme of life. The American Revolution, which so greatly influenced him by psychological need and propaganda requirement, had exhibited the phenomenon. The myth of the Revolution, which de Valera had absorbed before his American journey in 1919, skated over the many inferior minds who had played their parts in the conflict and the new regime. And had not 1916, like 1776, been also a revolution of the intellectuals? De Valera had been brought into it by an intellectual, Thomas MacDonagh, who may not have been of Jeffersonian or Hamiltonian stature, but there was not a poet or critic in Revolutionary America to touch him. Pearse and Connolly had been intellectuals: de Valera had known them, if not well. He would hardly have considered that the real Irish revolution, the one of 1919-21, had been much more the revolution of the anti-intellectuals, to judge by the performances of many of them when they came into power. He could see that the new and vigorous minds trained in the National University of Ireland or in his own

Blackrock had a capacity for fulfilling themselves which the shadow of a British state would deny them, had denied him.

These ideas, while not formally articulated, must have supplied him with a rationale for the situation in which he found himself as he shaped his thought for American responses from 1916 to 1919. His sense of the sanctity of the Irish Volunteers' legacy gave him no alternative in his first exercise in formal cabinet-making, that of Dáil Éireann in April 1919, and here in any case he was bound by what had been nominated and elected during his time in Lincoln Gaol, not to speak of Brugha's dispositions during his Acting Presidency. He also had to consider the politics of coalition under which he had been elected President of Sinn Féin, and cultivate the several different loyalties of his followers many of whom had accepted him as a common denominator rather than a first choice. (He had not, of course, been their lowest common denominator.) His cabinet reshuffle in 1921 had simply varied the available mixture.

The Cosgrave government did broaden its Cabinet base beyond the gunmen and their immediate secular wing. For instance, it brought in John Marcus O'Sullivan, Professor of Modern History in University College Dublin. And its own composition had naturally reflected the element of lawyers and professional men who might have been expected to accept the Treaty as the best available bargain instead of maintaining an ideological virginity as prescribed by Mary MacSwiney. The ice had, nevertheless, restrained their development along normal political lines. They virtually required an unspoken approval, a type of *post facto* participation, from their supporters, in their severity during the Civil War, and their new recruits had to partake of that sacrament. De Valera on his side saw himself as even more limited in his choices. He did accept new recruits, but they also had to witness the righteousness of his cause and see that righteousness as the core of their political being. Beyond that, the native distrust of his fellow-creatures inspired in de Valera by his infancy and youth, meant that he absolutely depended on persons whose loyalty to him had been proved again and again. In return, he had to give them loyalty beyond all political norms.

The word 'feudal' might give a clue to the relationship, but is both too liberal and too modern. He would have seen their fealty and his obligations as those of clansmen and chief, with a hugely idealistic notion as to how the ancient relationship between clansmen and chief was observed. De Valera had read the old bards, or at least their modern translators, and took from their expressions of devout love and fidelity a social norm: MacLiag's lament for Kincora (Brian Boru's seat) or O'Hussey's ode to the Maguire as rendered into the English of James Clarence Mangan emphatically became what every schoolboy knew in de Valera's Ireland. This might seem to accord little with the personality of, say, Seán Lemass, but it was not entirely fanciful. MacEntee had written poems of fallen chieftains, including one for MacDonagh:

> His cup of doom he drank, as one might quaff
> A bumper toast 'mid friends and merry chaff . . .

The result was that de Valera's Cabinet government was primarily limited to persons of two kinds: his immediate political followers through his vicissitudes, and those of the Irish Republican Army higher command who had followed him into Fianna Fáil. To them were added the relatives of other martyrs. This was no longer mere sacred symbolism, as though promoting a relative amounted to elevating a human relic; for rank-and-file constituency nominations it would be, but the Cabinet reliance on martyrs' kin was based on memories of deep affection. Gerry Boland came in as Harry Boland's brother, Erskine Childers the younger was groomed from 1932 for a place as the son of his father, but de Valera had loved Harry Boland, and revered Erskine Childers. When in 1957 it was felt that Gerry (appointed Minister for Posts and Telegraphs 1933, transferred to Lands 1936, and thence to Justice 1939) should make way for younger blood, the 71-year-old lieutenant was bitterly wounded, and the hurt was only eased when his 74-year-old leader explained that he would be succeeded at Justice by his son Kevin, a freshman elected in that year's crop. The year 1957 had been a bumper election victory for Fianna Fáil, but it was quite unprecedented for de Valera to choose a Minister from the new arrivals—indeed the only previous such appointment had been the slightly ominous precedent of Dr Noël Browne in the first Costello Coalition. Youth, however, would be served, provided it had relatives who had sacrificed themselves either by death or seniority. It would be idle to remark that nothing in Mr Kevin Boland's future career justified this confidence in his abilities, and indeed that much would call it into question. He was not being appointed for his abilities. De Valera was still a priest-king, and the sacerdotal requirements were fulfilled genealogically in Kevin Boland's somewhat bovine person. Gerry Boland may, of course, have thought of himself as young blood: he had been first appointed to the Cabinet a mere twenty-four years before 1957 whereas Lemass, Aiken, MacEntee and Ryan had been Ministers since 1932.

The Irish Roman Catholic clergy are famed for their enthusiasm for building and administration. Gerry Boland's priestship had initially involved the critical work of co-Secretaryship with Seán Lemass in the building of Fianna Fáil. The appointment of his son carried with it the presumption that he might pass on to him some of the secrets of his calling, or at least refrain from passing them on to a wider audience. Gerry Boland did give a major newspaper reporter the story of his career, ultimately, but not until Lemass was out of office. Maintenance in office was a check on the past, and secrecy for its own sake was a hallmark of the de Valera government. It was characteristic of him that he extended his own approach to life to his reign.

Cosgrave in his ten years had weathered or invited several major resignations, and had demoted two Ministers to lower office. De Valera in his twenty-one hardly got rid of anyone. Those who went seem to have gone in almost all instances at their own volition. In one way he must have felt he had no alternative. Having started as a forger and symbol of coalition separatist nationalist politics, he had gone through split after split, first from the Treatyites, then from Sinn Féin. He could not permit even the slightest risk of another major schism. But his own search for approval dictated by his youth meant that, at the heart of his government, he had to have something far beyond normal patterns of party loyalty. He responded by giving his subordinates as much personal freedom as was compatible with his overall direction and their common harmony. His own instincts lay entirely against interventionist government: witness de Valera's remark to the Dáil on 1 March 1946, evidently uttered with genuine regret: 'The Government, and legislation generally, have nowadays to intervene very much in what would be regarded as the private concerns of the individual.'[16] He believed passionately in the restoration of the Irish language; but apart from Government tests for civil servants he insisted that it had to be the people who did the work, not the Government. A Government printing and publication office disseminated large numbers of works in translation. In fact, de Valera's natural instinct to believe in what he wanted to believe, beginning with Mother-love, led him into what Conor Cruise O'Brien has termed 'a desperate game of "let's pretend"'.[17] Irish was declared the first language by the Constitution. Teaching was decreed by the monolingual method: facing pages in Irish and English would have been a far surer means of instilling the language into those who did not have it, but this conviction that Government must not dictate, and his desire to ensure the language was restored, led to the fiction that it had been restored—a bilingual form of reading instruction would be acknowledgement that the restoration had been less than complete. In response to crises of unemployment, similarly, de Valera answered by exhortation. The Dublin slums and beggars remained one of the horrors of his Ireland to the day of his retirement.

But if Ministers wanted to be interventionist and could justify their proposals to the cabinet, that was another matter. Lemass built on the precedents for 'semi-state' bodies in the Cosgrave government to push through a set of the most advanced forms of state intervention in history while Minister for Industry and Commerce in the 1930s: the Industrial Credit Company, the Irish Life Assurance Board, Industrial Alcohol Factories Ltd, the fuel board, the national airline, the Tourist Board. He moved into deeper direction of the Electricity Supply Board, the railways, sugar refining, and cement. The Jeffersonian de Valera clearly did not intend that the fame of his first governments would depend chiefly on the Department of Industry and Commerce, but he gave Lemass credit for producing the goods. It may be that on the evidence of a somewhat hysterical letter from Lemass to the cabinet on 7 November 1932 there is reason to conclude de Valera from the first saw the need to contain him by as much flexibility as possible: Lemass, faced with the Irish Free State's weakness in a depression-saturated world, declared that they faced 'a crisis as grave as that of 1847'[18]—the heart of the Great Famine—and demanded the end of the economic war with which the abolition of the oath and the cancellation of the annuities were leading the British to respond. De Valera saw his electoral credibility depending on the elimination of the oath and the relic of ancient landlord tyranny. His economic nationalism was in fact, ironically, the mood of the time: Roosevelt followed suit the next year. Lemass himself quickly learned to make the most of it. The original fuel for it emerged from one of the time-seams in the ice. De Valera could draw on the thought of the dead Griffith, a great advocate of economic protectionism, and use the ground that Griffith's evangelism had prepared: in fact, his administration proved much more true to Griffith's economic philosophy than did Griffith's own successors among the pro-Treaty Ministers. Similarly, consensus politics were achieved across time by Lemass's building on the work of McGilligan, but the co-operation remained one of past with present, not of Government with Opposition.

It was not only the forceful and impatient Lemass whose zeal had to be harnessed. Of de Valera's initial team the specifically urban figures were all favourable to state intervention: Lemass, MacEntee, Seán T. Ó Ceallaigh. They might—and did—argue like fury about the means it should take, but they agreed on the principle. De Valera found the old IRA leaders tended to be more in keeping with his Arcadian vision: Frank Aiken, Tom Derrig, P.J. Ruttledge, Oscar Traynor. Of these, Aiken became his closest confidant. But this was less a meeting of minds than a form of co-worship. Aiken was a good listener, a pleasant and likeable figure, and embodied the transition to de Valera of the Republican leadership from Liam Lynch, whom Aiken had succeeded. Lynch had led the IRA with little reference to de Valera; his successor ensured that de Valera was sanctified by the blood of the martyrs. It is just possible that his close links with de Valera arose from his proximity to areas where de Valera's political conscience might be most tender. Aiken had seriously tried to mediate on the eve of Civil War, although he had eventually thrown in his lot with the anti-Treaty forces. He came from rural Armagh: he joined the Irish Volunteers in 1913, he was not prominent in Sinn Féin, but had fought in the Northern Command, during the Anglo-Irish war. Aiken was Minister for Defence in the 1930s, which meant that he had to keep a watchful eye on any threats against the Government from his old friends in the IRA as well as being vigilant against disaffection in the state's armed forces which might stem from pro-Treaty activists. But he was made wartime Minister for the Co-ordination of Defensive Measures during the war, with Oscar Traynor replacing him as Minister for Defence, which some interpreted as a measure to prevent his becoming a risk on Northern Ireland. He had hopes of activity against Northern Ireland before he left the IRA to follow de Valera. Yet, although he was credited with stiffening anti-British sentiment in de Valera's mind, it is unlikely: Aiken was receptive in his own mind rather than an influence on others. He seems to have had enthusiasm for the Social Credit views of Major C.H. Douglas, and he later was interested in Keynesian economics, but it was left to the First Costello Coalition to introduce Ireland's first Keynesian budget, at the hands of McGilligan.[19]

There was a boyish quality in Aiken, so that he supplied a friendship which was psychologically very valuable to de Valera. Lemass, MacEntee, Ryan, and to a lesser extent the other Ministers were more public friendships. De Valera's cabinet methods throughout his career are agreed to have been very curious. His followers were bound to him by deep ties of loyalty, in most instances of affection also, and in most cases their political success was unthinkable without him. Yet he seldom seems to have tried to overawe them. His procedure was always to allow meetings to continue, at times it seemed interminably, rather than go to a vote. It was not that he simply wanted to exhaust opposition, although from his American mission to his appointment of the 25-man Vocational Organization Commission he showed how well he knew the value of unlimited talk to prevent unwanted action.

De Valera was not a mental sadist, battening on more stupid associates.

His use of the talking-out tactic was in general a defensive one. He was unsure of himself and his acceptability. He found it a good means to distance vociferous opposition, and take stock of a new situation and new negotiators or protagonists. He played a part of self-assurance, but he was constantly undermined by outside events in that self-assurance until he formed his first Government. To him what was critical was unity under his leadership: this did not mean unity under his dictation. He did not seek to provoke and demolish disagreement, but to allow disagreement to dispose of itself. His Dáil Cabinet, in 1921, was ultimately split irrevocably and disastrously, and he must have realized that its fate was in part caused by the personal feud between Stack and Brugha, on the one side, and Collins on the other. He ended up on the side of Stack and Brugha, but at least initially he had not expected to: and his departure from Sinn Féin in 1926 meant a parting of the ways from Stack. Above all, his need to be accepted meant that the team's unity was required to reassure him again and again. But he could not give the clue to this weakness. He also recognized that the two most remarkable men on his team, Lemass and MacEntee, were the two most frequently at loggerheads: he had no wish to restrain the talents of either of them. Nor do his choices reflect a search for inferiors appointed to be overawed. Lemass, MacEntee, Ó Ceallaigh and, outside the Cabinet, Briscoe, all possessed what might best be described as a kind of Irish Cockney perkiness, iconoclastic and down-to-earth. If de Valera was most relaxed with Aiken, he enjoyed the contrasting style of the urbanites as a refreshment, not as a target.[20]

One casualty from his political life lay in the disappearance of the Revolutionary women. His Constitution of 1937 was his personal declaration of independence in this respect. Constance Markiewicz died in 1927, Pearse's mother in 1932, both safe in the arms of Fianna Fáil. But they were not to have successors. Margaret Pearse inherited her mother's place in the movement, but de Valera's control of her was absolute in political terms. The fate of the Pearses symbolized de Valera's success in moving women from a place of control to one of support. He had been so successful with Mrs Pearse that in 1925 she had publicly requested John Devoy never to mention her sons' names in public again. Her daughter would be limited to purely Irish appearances at party rallies and in the Senate, but her place as priestess of the shrine was secure. Correspondingly, Mrs Tom Clarke, also in Fianna Fáil, fell increasingly from favour. She had sheltered de Valera in her house during the Civil War, and her regard was vital to him professionally and personally until 1932. But with his mother's death the need to have the approval of her Irish counterparts diminished drastically. He received an unpleasant reminder that the Republican women could use family bereavement in an attempt to put him in his place when Hanna Sheehy-Skeffington wrote a vigorous obituary of the late Catherine Wheelwright for Peadar O'Donnell's *An Phoblacht,* Socialist as well as irreconcilably Republican in 1932: Mrs Sheehy-Skeffington had become friends with the old lady during her visits to America, an alliance all the more formidable because of their common confidence in their forceful rectitude. His mother dead no longer needed his proofs of his worthiness of acceptance. She was with God, in Whom de Valera had far more confidence of support than he did from Hanna Sheehy-Skeffington or Kathleen Clarke.

Her death may have been an absolute turning-point in his views on women in the movement. He came into conflict in the legislature with Mrs Clarke on his relegation of women to the fireside by the Constitution. He was very forceful about it: on 11 May 1937 in the Dáil he declared 'I believe that ninety-nine per cent of the women of this country will agree with every line of this'. And later in that speech:

> Are we to go back to the beginning of the industrial era? Are we, through our law and through the regulations made under these laws, to make certain that the inadequate strength of women shall not be abused? Where is the derogation from the rights of women in that?

Mrs Clarke went on from this issue to the Constitution's inadequacy as an instrument of separation from Britain, asserting that at the time of de Valera's unsuccessful reform of Sinn Féin in 1926 he had told her of:

> the dangers inherent in the change; if we succeeded, it was possible that all the place-hunting professional politician element would swarm into the organization and the Republican element would be swamped, and that would leave the leaders in a very weak position to carry out their programme.

De Valera at the Fianna Fáil Árd-Fheis on 12 October 1937 was ruthless in reply:

> Mrs Clarke today said her mind was a hell; that she had troubles because she saw the leaders slipping and slipping. She repeats some conversation that I am supposed to have had when Fianna Fáil was founded. I have a fair idea of the sort of words I would use. I have been looking over the report of that conversation as given, and the words are not the sort of words I am in the habit of using.[21]

It was his version of the lie direct. The break from his dependence on mother-figures was absolute. In the end Mrs Clarke broke with de Valera and defected to MacBride, in whose cause she obtained a pitiful handful of votes in the 1948 election, her party putting her last on the list of its nominees in Dublin North-East. Perhaps de Valera had spoken for 99 per cent of the women of Ireland after all. As for Mrs Clarke, her supersession as high priestess of the Easter Rising by Senator Margaret Pearse was virtually a proof that de Valera had succeeded in what Stalin merely threatened, when in his disagreements with Krupskaya he declared he would make someone else Lenin's official widow.

Women were relegated, then, and in part de Valera's new position meant, here as in so much else, that he had tacitly accepted the views of his hated, discredited and displaced Opposition. Just as the struggle for national separation had swept the cause of Socialism into subservience, it also swept that of feminism; and then the female idealism exploited by the men became the means of proving their egregiousness. De Valera had been drawn under feminist magnetism by more subtle psychological pressures, but once these disappeared he was as thankful to relegate them to the fireside as the bitterest of their pro-Treaty critics.[22]

Mrs Tom Clarke's fears, which de Valera so ungraciously declined to admit having shared, raise the question of how far professional politics altered the nature of the movement, and specifically of de Valera himself. In the short term she was wrong. De Valera did not change his views dramatically for reasons of party politics; his reasons for change, as on the women question, were much more personal as a rule. When in his last meeting with Liam Lynch early in 1923 he had tried to sway the anti-Treaty guerrilla leader towards cessation of hostilities, he countered Lynch's query as to what Tom Clarke would think of laying down the struggle with the reply (as he recalled it to the editor he had chosen for his newspaper, the *Irish Press,* Frank Gallagher) 'Tom Clarke is dead'.[23] De Valera simply returned to his normal outlook. He would no longer allow the past to dominate him, he would dominate it. Lynch, for his part, followed Tom Clarke. As for the professional politicians, Mrs Clarke's recollection deserved more courtesy, but what de Valera had probably said to her was that he realized the dangers, thereby implying that he would take measures accordingly.

Nor does he seem to have seen his party swamped by professionals to the detriment of his leadership and the acceptance of his ideals. He never intended his party to become a Frankenstein monster, and during his life in politics it did not. From Gerry Boland and Seán Lemass to Tommy Mullins, the party bosses served and did not dare to command. It was only when de Valera announced he would stand for the Presidency that things changed. First, there was the crass attempt to abolish Proportional Representation, unsuccessfully linked to his apotheosis. The 1966 campaign for his re-election as President lost him votes by Fianna Fáil's blatant attempt to make party capital of it. De Valera had seen the Presidency under his Constitution as honorific: he had underlined as much by the choice of Dr Douglas Hyde as his first nominee in 1938 (an interesting *amende honorable* for Hyde's ouster from the Gaelic League Presidency by those who drew de Valera from his first public commitment). In 1966 he paid the price for having allowed the ice to make the contest a party one after Hyde's retirement in 1945, when Ó Ceallaigh had been put up, defeating Fine Gael's General Seán Mac Eoin. But the 1966 campaign put the party wheelhorses in command: Ó Ceallaigh's nomination had been a manifestation of what T.H. White so aptly termed 'the holy will of Dev'.[24] Any obeisance to party political machine men when he was Taoiseach would have involved promoting young blood. In fact, de Valera seldom even consulted his Ministers about Cabinet changes, including their own. Lemass asked in 1951 that MacEntee, then very unpopular in the country, be taken from Finance. De Valera acceded to his request—in 1957. The changes in Government brought about under Lemass was the proof of machine politics finding its demands being met then, and only then. De Valera was left to reflect on the effects when during the Arms trial in 1970 he is said to have opined that Charles J. Haughey would one day destroy the party. It is said to have been by his wish that Frank Aiken retired from politics in 1973 in protest against the selection of Haughey for Dáil candidacy once more. Aiken was, after all, only 75 at that juncture, and de Valera had stayed as Taoiseach two more years beyond that, to say nothing of fourteen more in the Presidency.[25]

But where lay power? De Valera made policy dependent on his formulae for agreement, not only at Cabinet level, but also in inter-Departmental policy-making. Professor Farrell has shown that this could result in such effects as a children's allowance scheme being proposed in 1939 and finally obtaining acceptance in 1944. Lemass made remarkable strides within his own Department of Industry and Commerce, and later in his wartime duty as Minister for Supplies. He did so, while his colleagues did what they did, under a reign much more in keeping with the American Presidency than the British premiership. An exceptional hold on power was therefore retained, not by the politicians, but by the civil service. De Valera had followed British rather than American practice in 1932 by refusing to tamper with the professional state administration. Even P.S. O'Hegarty, as Secretary for the Department of Posts and Telegraphs, retained his position despite having only eight years before expressed his opinion of the new head of Government in a chapter of *The Victory of Sinn Féin* smartly captioned 'Devil Era', and another specifically mentioning de Valera in the title while flourishing as its epigraph the final lines of Pope's *Dunciad:*

> Thy hand, great Anarch! lets the curtain fall;
> And Universal Darkness buries All.

There would be commentators to maintain, long after, that this in fact was a fair description not of de Valera's responsibility for the Civil War, which for all of O'Hegarty's eloquence was much less than that of many others, but of the reign of a Head of Government who left so much of the direction of state in the hands of O'Hegarty and his colleagues in the civil service.

De Valera required that the civil service sink itself in anonymity, and this subordination of their personalities into their office to the extent that personal publication of any kind had usually to be pseudonymous (when not in the Irish language and hence harmless), meant that anonymity became the cloak for self-defence. The civil service, in general, developed a resistance to change whose ultimate effects were alarming. In particular the Irish Department of Finance under J.J. McElligott maintained an icy resistance to any proposals for change which might entail public expenditure, in the finest traditions of the British Treasury. It was not until the appointment of T.K. Whitaker as McElligott's second successor that Finance began to show what it could do in the direction of constructive, well-moving national planning, and that took place in 1956 under the Second Costello Coalition. But Whitaker's proposals for advocacy of lines of economic development were given the go-ahead by de Valera's last Minister for Finance, James Ryan. Elsewhere, for instance in education, the cold resistance to reform was buttressed by a judicious deployment of national icons. It never seemed to occur to Ministers and civil servants that apart from the highly arid interpretation of nationalism officially declared to be shovelled forth to the schoolchildren, they were perpetuating what Pearse had so bitterly attacked in his eloquent pamphlet on education 'The Murder Machine'. In Agriculture the resistance to change was peculiarly pernicious: developments in livestock improvement, for instance, were not only discouraged but positively proscribed, inspectors tramping the country to make sure that no examples of the Landrace pig were being introduced in place of 'the official pig'. Occasional exercises in public relations to counter criticism induced a bitter cynicism: it was said in the early 1950s that since *Scéim na Muc* (the pig-scheme) had been proposed, the grunt of a pig had been heard in one Opposition Deputy's county as frequently as a heckler at a closed Fianna Fáil meeting.

De Valera himself obtained excellent staff-work and maintained it, with his devoted private secretary, Kathleen O'Connell, and his charming, boyish Secretary to the Government, Maurice Moynihan. It was of course supportive, and was intended by him to be. He had settled into his ways when Moynihan took up his post in 1937; the Constitution was de Valera's last major piece of initiation. For the rest, his was the posture of guarding the gains, defending what his men might secure, just as he had begun his political nationalism by rallying to the Irish Volunteers in a defensive spirit. His affirmation of his Arcadian ideals and his martyrological custodianship, in one form or another, had an inspirational dignity. De Valera was self-sacrificing to a degree in his presence at an endless succession of funerals of persons who had played one part or another in the national movement. His tall, black-clad form mingled among the mourners with no attempt to take limelight from the corpse, something very unusual among heads of government. He might claim—though he did not—that the cultural desert which his country was fast becoming was the work of other hands than his. If intellectual enquiry in the Universities was severely restricted, the repressive Board of Trinity College Dublin was Unionist, the tyrannical President of University College Dublin was Fine Gael, the noisy literary censorship and the obscurantist pressure groups on public morals were not his creatures. But there was little difference between their values and his, save that he was no witch-hunter.

The ice was at its most evident in the awful aridity of politics. The ex-gunmen in the Cabinet—Derrig, Ruttledge, Oscar Traynor—set a pattern in cautious mediocrity. To de Valera's credit it must be said that while he above all perpetuated the ice, his influence remained a quietly healthy check against snobbery, as in Britain, or the eruption of demagogic Red scares, as in the United States. An occasional figure might mushroom into political prominence, such as Oliver Flanagan, the anti-Semitic sole Deputy of the Monetary Reform party in the early 1940s, but de Valera's exhibition of public friendship for Briscoe and ultimate instruction for him to seek the Dublin Lord Mayoralty were the king-priestly means of ensuring that Ireland was never in his day disgraced by anti-Semitism of the kind notorious in Irish-America. His prominent use of Childers in the party was a signal of his liking for good relations between Catholic and Protestant. So was the choice of Douglas Hyde as the first President under his Constitution.

These things were in some degree shop-window work to underline contrasts with Northern Ireland, and in their effect they were less successful than his affection for Briscoe; he was not entirely blameless in that, for the incessant repetition of the wrongs of Irish Catholics in times past as luridly retold in his newspapers deepened the cleavage between the Christian religions. And the same emphasis on past wrongs inevitably gave fuel to the youthful zealots who reappeared with monotonous regularity in successive generations to initiate violent actions ostensibly to assert their hostility to Northern Ireland, actually—did they but know it—to register their protest against the futility which martyrological politics had become.

He should never have remained as head of government in the 1950s. Yet defeat made it impossible for him to quit. His return to power in 1951 was only made possible by the votes of Dr Noël Browne and his supporters who had been driven out of the coalition by the pusillanimity of Costello and the treachery of MacBride. He was defeated again in 1954. But he got his clear majority in 1957, and once more all was well. The people were where they should be. He had won once again the acceptance which meant so much to him, had won it indisputably, and thanks only to his own. He may also have been influenced in the early 1950s by his old adversary Winston Churchill clinging to power. No doubt he felt that it was necessary to ensure the full agreement of Aiken, Ryan and MacEntee in the choice of Lemass, and, as usual, he was prepared to allow protracted debate to achieve accord.

At last he announced his departure, and it says much for his hypnotism of his country that it fell like a thunderclap on the public. Then there were the ceremonial years in the Presidency, when the ice closed on him as well as regards any indication of his views on the whirlwind leadership of Lemass. He performed his work with supreme dignity in Ireland when Kennedy came, and in the United States when Kennedy died. He returned two years later and at last won the accolade for which in 1919–20 he had looked in vain, that of following in Parnell's footsteps by addressing the US Congress. He paid his lifetime's debt to the intellectual leadership of Woodrow Wilson, regardless of Wilson's cavalier treatment of his own mission, and congratulated the United States on having begotten the League of Nations. He would have taken great pride in his choice of place for finally settling his account with Devoy, Cohalan and Hiram Johnson, whose ghost must have been sorely tried by this blasphemy in his own isolationist stamping-ground.

He served out his two terms, returned to his little house in Cross Avenue, Blackrock, and must have been pleased when he was succeeded by the son of his old friend Erskine Childers. But young Childers died in office, very suddenly in 1974. Lemass had gone too, in 1971, having retired as early as 1966. On 7 January 1975 came the worst loss of all: Sinéad. Now he wanted no delay. And on 29 August, he followed her.

In a sense, Shaw had written *Saint Joan* about him, or at least about those he supported, when the play was being constructed in Kerry in 1923. The idea of rejection of a pragmatic political settlement on a question of identity is basic to the play, and became basic to de Valera, perhaps even on the point of his own Presidency. Like Joan, he was open to the reproach of being proud and disobedient: it is her former friend the Archbishop who says it to her, as it was de Valera's former friends the Bishops who said it to him. This study has looked at some of the origins of this Joan, and charts a divergence from much of Shaw. Dr John Bowman's deeply thoughtful *De Valera and the Ulster Question* (Oxford, 1982), sets the conflicting interpretations of his career at the outset:

> A revolutionary nationalist who defined his goal in the 1916 Easter Rising in Dublin and spent the rest of his long career working for the achievement of a united, sovereign Irish Republic; or, the first of the revisionists, a complex, secretive, essentially conservative politician who often concealed his political strategy from his colleagues and, consciously, from history?[26]

Underneath the part he played, de Valera had to try to bring together his shattered loyalties, to the point of deceiving himself: and that self-deception dictated by his yearnings for acceptance by his mother and his search for identification with his father, gave him a lifetime's habit of self-deception. The part he was forced to play had its trappings which he could never renounce. But the Ireland he sought to build was an ideal extension of his own Bruree, not any attempt to realize what a unified Ireland must include, especially in Ulster. Above all, he appeared to his contemporaries a divisive and factious figure: yet his own instinct was one to win approval, acceptance, affirmation. Circumstances thrust him into conflict, physical and political. His reaction was to strengthen his links with those elements still accepting him, and freeze the rest into ice, so that the imaginary wider unity he insisted on could be said to have been achieved. His first real friend, the Catholic church, gave him an identity larger than himself. Having seen how its panoply supported him, he borrowed its forms to maintain his identity. His revisionism was thus revisionism by stealth, almost intended to conceal itself from himself. On the other hand, his conservatism was apparent enough, and consistent with the crisis of his early years: he wanted a return to an Ireland in which mothers did not go away. What he had acquired in security so painfully he did not want to risk, although time and again he was forced to risk it. The Easter Rising gave him a means of winning acceptance, but on terms he had to appear to maintain, alien to him though many of them were. He seemed the most self-assured statesman of his time; in many ways he had the least basis for self-assurance.

This investigation may have come closer to resolving some of his contradictions, but it is the curse of revisionism that it seems to chip so much away that it sometimes seems almost impossible to retain a sense of the original reality. We strip away the myth; we may be left with a vacuum at the kernel. For the myth itself supplies a reality.

De Valera maintained the neutrality of Éire throughout the Second World War, ostensibly because of the partition of Ireland. In fact, the extent of anti-British feeling among some of his own former, and even present, supporters, meant that any involvement in war on the British (or, obviously, the German) side would have split the country asunder. Moreover, had Ireland entered the war, beleaguered Britain would never have been able to give it sufficient defence, and the Germans would probably have obtained a foothold which could have been disastrous for Britain as well as Eire. De Valera, true to his international as well as his defensive instincts, had planned carefully for the war, was here well supported by his civil service, and had even worked out means for preserving Irish identity should a successful invasion capture Dublin and cut off his Government from the people. So little was Irish partition the key to de Valera's policy that he rejected any Allied blandishments on the question to draw him into the war. The emergency Government sat tight and waited for invasion; it sustained a little bombing, and it intervened to bring fire-fighting assistance to Belfast during the terrible bombing raids there. When the United States entered the war, pressures of a different kind were brought to bear on Ireland. A hostile United States Ambassador even reflected at one point on overthrowing the de Valera government and perhaps putting an Irish or American general in control. De Valera, conscious of the clear commitment of the people to neutrality, resisted all attempts to persuade him to join the Allied cause even at the point of clear and certain victory. On the other hand, he had given a good deal of secret support to the Allies, much more than almost any of his people knew. The famous British myth about Irish lights facilitating German submarines conflicts with the reality of which the Dominions Secretary, Lord Cranborne, informed the British Cabinet at the war's end: lights had been doused when the British requested it. Captured Allied personnel had been restored to the war theatre.

At all events, Winston Churchill let himself go in a broadcast on 13 May 1945. It contained reckless and brutal charges about de Valera's having frolicked with the Axis diplomats throughout the war, stating that only an extraordinary forbearance had held the Allies' hand from a well-justified invasion of Éire. Its implications were unjust and untrue, and he must have known them to be untrue. Three days later de Valera replied in a broadcast on Radio Éireann. It is the greatest single moment of his career, and he unquestionably spoke for a united people of the twenty-six counties. For once, the ice melted in support behind him. And he, so much cast as the man of war, gave with characteristic pedagogic simplicity a supreme example in the meaning and making of Peace.

> Certain newspapers have been very persistent in looking for my answer to Mr Churchill's recent broadcast. I know the kind of answer I am expected to make. I know the answer that first springs to the lips of every man of Irish blood who heard or read that speech, no matter in what circumstances or in what part of the world he found himself.
>
> I know the reply I would have given a quarter of a century ago. But I have deliberately decided that that is not the reply I shall make tonight. I shall strive not to be guilty of adding any fuel to the flames of hatred and passion which, if continued to be fed, promise to burn up whatever is left by the war of decent human feeling in Europe.
>
> Allowances can be made for Mr Churchill's statement, however unworthy, in the first flush of his victory. No such excuse could be found for me in this quieter atmosphere. There are, however, some things which it is my duty to say, some things which it is essential to say. I shall try to say them as dispassionately as I can.
>
> Mr Churchill makes it clear that, in certain circumstances, he would have violated our neutrality and that he would justify his action by Britain's necessity. It seems strange to me that Mr Churchill does not see that this, if accepted, would mean that Britain's necessity would become a moral code and that when this necessity became sufficiently great, other people's rights were not to count.
>
> It is quite true that other great powers believe in this same code—in their own regard—and have behaved in accordance with it. That is precisely why we have the disastrous succession of wars—World War No. 1 and World War No. 2—and shall it be World War No. 3?
>
> Surely Mr Churchill must see that, if his contention be admitted in our regard, a like justification can be framed for similar acts of aggression elsewhere and no small nation adjoining a great power could ever hope to be permitted to go its own way in peace.
>
> It is, indeed, fortunate that Britain's necessity did not reach the point when Mr Churchill would have acted. All credit to him that he successfully resisted

the temptation which, I have no doubt, many times assailed him in his difficulties and to which I freely admit many leaders might have easily succumbed. It is, indeed, hard for the strong to be just to the weak, but acting justly always has its rewards.

By resisting his temptation in this instance, Mr Churchill, instead of adding another horrid chapter to the already bloodstained record of the relations between England and this country, has advanced the cause of international morality an important step—one of the most important, indeed, that can be taken on the road to the establishment of any sure basis for peace. . . .[27]

Notes

Notes to Chapter 1

[1] Ruth Dudley Edwards, *Patrick Pearse: The Triumph of Failure* (London, 1977), pp. 323–44.

[2] Michael Oakeshott, *The Social and Political Doctrines of Contemporary Europe* (Cambridge, 1939), pp. xx, 45, 72–77.

[3] Maureen Wall, *The Penal Laws 1691–1760: Church and State from the Treaty of Limerick to the Accession of George III.* (Dundalk, 1961), *passim.*

Notes to Chapter 2

[1] Sir C.F.N. Macready, *Annals of an Active Life* (London, 1924), II. p. 574.

[2] These and subsequent details of de Valera's early life are all from: Maurice Moynihan ed., *Speeches and Statements by Eamon de Valera* (Dublin and New York, 1980), p. xxxiii; Tomás Ó Néill agus Pádraig Ó Fiannachta, *De Valera* (Dublin, 1968), I. pp. 1–29; The Earl of Longford and Thomas P. O'Neill, *Eamon de Valera* (London, 1970), pp. 1–50; and above all Seán P. Farragher, CSSP, *Dev and his Alma Mater: Eamon de Valera's Lifelong Association with Blackrock College 1898–1975* (Dublin, 1984), pp. 5–117, and documents reproduced therein. Mary Bromage, *De Valera and the March of a Nation* (London, 1956), *passim,* supplies a few additional details. A very enthusiastic obituary of de Valera's mother which centres on an incident when she was campaigning for her son's release in early 1917 and indicates her powers of organization and iron will was contributed by Hanna Sheehy-Skeffington to *An Phoblacht,* 25 June 1932.

[3] Farragher, *Dev and his Alma Mater,* p. 8: 'Note about his father entered by Dev in the Bible he won as a prize at Blackrock', reproduced.

[4] Longford and O'Neill, *de Valera,* pp. 471–72. It is my understanding that these words are Professor O'Neill's.

[5] Ibid., p. 5.

[6] T.P. O'Connor and Robert McWade, *Gladstone, Parnell and the Great Irish Struggle* (Sydney, NSW, 1886), p. 506. William O'Brien and Desmond Ryan, eds., *Devoy's Post Bag 1871–1928* (Dublin, 1953), pp. 352–54.

[7] 'I have in my possession a yellowed photograph of my great-uncle which President de Valera gave me with the words, "*Eisean a mhúin an tír ghrá dham*". (He taught me patriotism)' (Conor Cruise O'Brien, *States of Ireland* (New York, 1972), p. 19). Sheehy's family are discussed in detail by his great-nephew in the same work.

[8] R.V. Comerford, *Charles J. Kickham–A Study in Irish nationalism and literature* (Dublin, 1979), pp. 198–200, 211. See also my remarks on Kickham in *Celtic Nationalism* (London, 1968), pp. 152–55.

[9] Seán O'Faoláin, *De Valera* (London, 1939), pp. 25–26. Sinéad's engagement to de Valera greatly annoyed one of her other pupils, his future pro-Treaty enemy Ernest Blythe, who when asked whom she was going out with now replied: 'Ah, some class of a mulatto called Demerara'. (Private information).

[10] On Sinéad in addition to fn. 2 above see Farragher, *Dev and his Alma Mater,* p. 176, also her own writings, some of which have been translated. For de Valera's bilingualism see Iris Dháil Éireann, Official Report, *Debate on the Treaty between Great Britain and Ireland* (Dublin, n.d.), p. 7. MacDonagh, *Literature in Ireland* (Dublin, 1916), p. 102.

[11] The authoritative account is in Donal McCartney, *The National University of Ireland and Éamon de Valera* (Dublin, 1983), pp. 20–24. The Senate of the National University also rejected Thomas MacDonagh's candidacy for the Professorship of English Literature at University College Galway around this time.

[12] De Valera found Father Sheehy sitting in front of him at the meeting.

[13] Dudley Edwards, *Pearse,* pp. 264–67. See also the memoir by his son Donagh MacDonagh (who, however, was an infant when he died, but who has excellent insights) in F.X. Martin ed., *Leaders and Men of the Easter Rising: Dublin 1916* (London, 1967), pp. 165–76, MacDonagh's poems and prose, and the compilation TV film for the series 'On Behalf of the Provisional Government' (RTE, 1966).

[14] Francis Sheehy-Skeffington, 'An Open Letter to Thomas MacDonagh', May 1915, in *1916: The Easter Rising* (London, 1968), pp. 149–52 (edited by Fergus Pyle and Owen Dudley Edwards). Of this letter Donagh MacDonagh said to Owen Sheehy-Skeffington 'your father was right and mine was wrong'.

[15] In addition to Dudley Edwards, *Pearse,* see Michael Tierney, *Eoin MacNeill Scholar and Man of Action* ed. F.X. Martin (Oxford, 1980), pp. 156–239; Maureen Wall, essays in Kevin B. Nowlan ed., *The Making of 1916* (Dublin, 1969), pp. 157–255; and the 'On Behalf of the Provisional Government' series, especially 'Ceannt'. Tierney, *MacNeill,* p. 181, disposes of some of de Valera's self-deceptions in retrospect as to what he knew.

[16] To sources in fn. 2 above add 'Mr Devileur's Prisoner' in Dudley Edwards and Pyle, *1916,* pp. 132–34; Desmond Ryan, *The Rising* (Dublin, 1949), pp. 187–202; G.A. Hayes-McCoy, 'A Military History of the 1916 Rising' in Nowlan, *Making of 1916,* pp. 258–62, 286–91, 300, and notes.

[17] De Valera, brief memo on time in Longford and O'Neill, *De Valera,* pp. 46–47. The version given in the preceding text (p. 45) is that de Valera thought the

message spurious and was only convinced of its genuineness after Nurse O'Farrell's departure. But her account (reprinted in Roger McHugh ed., *Dublin 1916* (London, 1966), p. 214) makes it clear that when subalterns of his identified her he accepted the document but refused to act without orders from MacDonagh. So the conference about the document after she left was not about its authenticity and thus must have involved a reversal of de Valera's refusal to act on it.

[18] MacDonagh believed that with Pearse and Connolly in enemy hands 'the chief command devolved on him, and no one else had any right to issue commands or enter into negotiations', apparently himself accepted the 'peace conference' story, and thought 'the country was up' (Piaras Mac Lochlainn, *Last Words—Letters and Statements of the Leaders Executed After Easter 1916* (Dublin, 1971), pp. 49–50). He made no known attempt to reach de Valera when with British assistance he went to see Ceannt, but de Valera was his subordinate, not his colleague. News of de Valera's surrender could have been known to Lowe and filtered through to MacDonagh to influence his decision in the hour before he surrendered himself, although it is by no means certain that Lowe received it quickly. In retrospect de Valera may have felt he let MacDonagh down. This would have given another reason for later assigning an importance to Pearse he certainly did not grant him at the time, and for convincing himself he acted on Pearse's surrender orders once convinced of their authenticity.

[19] On Maxwell, see Sir George Arthur, *General Sir John Grenfell Maxwell* (London, 1932). On American intervention, see my 'American Aspects of the Rising' in Dudley Edwards and Pyle, *1916*, p. 162. Sir Shane Leslie asserted to his dying day that de Valera was saved by the intervention of Cardinal Gibbons in a direct appeal to the British Government (see e.g. his 'review' of F. Scott Fitzgerald, *This Side of Paradise, Dublin Review* (1920), p. 289). Gibbons was strongly pro-Ally.

Notes to Chapter 3

[1] Longford and O'Neill, *De Valera*, pp. 51–61. Ó Néill agus O Fiannachta, *De Valera*, I, pp. 67–87, and plates XI–XIII. Tierney, *MacNeill*, pp. 240–59. Robert Kee, *The Green Flag* (London, 1972), pp. 591–600.

[2] Fitzpatrick, 'De Valera in 1917: the Undoing of the Easter Rising' in John P. O'Carroll and John A. Murphy eds., *De Valera and his Times* (Cork, 1983), pp. 101–12; also Fitzpatrick, *Politics and Irish Life 1913–21—Provincial experience of war and revolution* (Dublin, 1977), a fascinating account of co. Clare. Tierney, *MacNeill*, pp. 259–62n. Sean Ó Lúing, *I Die in a Good Cause* (Tralee, 1970), discusses Ashe. Kevin J. Browne, *De Valera and the Banner County* (Dublin, 1982) gives the election in detail.

[3] Moynihan, *Speeches by de Valera*, p. 8. The speech explains that they had set up an Irish Republic 'to get international recognition' after which 'the Irish people may by referendum freely choose their own forms of government'.

[4] Brian M. Walker ed., *Parliamentary Election Results in Ireland, 1801–1922* (Dublin, 1978), p. 185. David W. Miller, *Church, State and Nation in Ireland, 1898–1921* (Dublin, 1973), pp. 403–05.

[5] Longford and O'Neill, *De Valera,* pp. 74–77.

[6] 'For the nationalist in the street . . . the struggle was for the substance of freedom and independence . . . it was neither necessary nor wise to claim that the people had voted uncompromisingly for "The Republic"' (John A. Murphy, *Ireland in the Twentieth Century* (Dublin, 1975), p. 7). The book is a major source of what follows.

[7] W. Alison Phillips, *The Revolution in Ireland 1906–1923* (London, 1923), p. 151.

[8] Charles Townshend, *The British Campaign in Ireland 1919–1921* (Oxford, 1975), pp. 16–20, is excellent on the beginning of the war: the whole book is packed with information and judicious analysis.

[9] John Bowman, *De Valera and the Ulster Question 1917–1973* (Oxford, 1982), pp. 29–43: a masterly assembly of material.

[10] Moynihan, *Speeches by de Valera,* p. 20.

[11] Unidentified newspaper reports, quoted in Desmond Ryan, *Unique Dictator* (London, 1936), pp. 99–100. I have returned it to direct speech.

[12] Longford and O'Neill, *De Valera,* pp. 97, 113. Sinéad de Valera to Michael Collins, 3 February 1922, in León Ó Broin ed., *In Great Haste—The Letters of Michael Collins and Kitty Kiernan* (Dublin, 1983), pp. 108–09 (translated by Dr Ó Broin from the original Irish). On the American mission in general I am deeply obliged to Professor O'Neill for a gift of ten years ago of *Ireland's Claim for Recognition as a Sovereign Independent State Presented Officially to the Government of the United States by Eamon de Valera President of the Irish Republic* (Washington, DC., n.d.), pp. 1–136.

[13] Longford and O'Neill, *De Valera,* p. 80.

[14] Moynihan, *Speeches by de Valera,* p. 28. Dr Moynihan quotes from a newspaper report whose earlier part is in indirect speech, which I have returned.

[15] Ibid., p. 29.

[16] Charles Callan Tansill, *America and the Fight for Irish Freedom 1866–1922* (New York, 1957), p. 342, quoting unidentified report from Cohalan MSS. Although this is the most bitter of many unfriendly analyses of the American mission, I have found its content indicative of arguments in de Valera's favour, once one discards Tansill's assumption that the only tenable positions for American public opinion were 'irreconcilable' anti-League or, the unspeakable, pro-British. For a sensitive and shrewd defence of de Valera by a source friendly to Devoy, see Desmond Ryan, *Unique Dictator,* pp. 102–32.

[17] Donal McCartney, 'De Valera in the United States' in Art Cosgrove and Donal McCartney eds., *Studies in Irish History Presented to R. Dudley Edwards* (Dublin, 1979), p. 323. I am sorry to disagree with this perceptive essay, especially in view of where it appeared, but Professor McCartney in my view overestimates the possibilities of Irish recognition by the USA and fails to see the dangers of an Irish involvement in Hiram Johnson's candidacy.

[18] C. Desmond Greaves, *Liam Mellows and the Irish Revolution* (London, 1971), pp. 210, 216.

[19] Moynihan, *Speeches by de Valera,* pp. 47–48. The speech also contains an unspecified but obvious reference to the Revolutionary hero Nathan Hale.

[20] León Ó Broin, *Revolutionary Underground—The Story of the Irish Republican Brotherhood 1858–1924* (Dublin, 1976), pp. 190–91: an invaluable book.

[21] Dorothy Macardle, *The Irish Republic* (London, 1937), p. 323.

[22] Lyons, *Ireland Since the Famine* (London, 1971), p. 419.

[23] Alison Phillips, *The Revolution in Ireland,* pp. 164–65.

[24] Tom Barry, *Guerrilla Days in Ireland* (Tralee, 1962: 1st edn., 1949), pp. 174–75.

[25] Dáil Éireann, *Private Sessions of Second Dáil* (Dublin, n.d.), p. 13.

[26] P.S. O'Hegarty, *The Victory of Sinn Féin—How it Won it, and How it Used it* (Dublin, 1924), pp. 86–87, quotes Griffith after the Treaty as saying de Valera used a mathematical diagram to show that 'External Association' was 'to bring Cathal along' to get out of 'the strait jacket of the Republic'. But it may also have been to draw Griffith away from his old loyalty to the idea of a dual monarchy, if the story is true.

[27] Wall, 'Partition: the Ulster Question (1916–1926)' in T. Desmond Williams, *The Irish Struggle 1916–1926* (London, 1966), p. 87. She points out that 'Of 338 pages of debate, nine only are devoted to the subject of partition'.

[28] Bowman, *De Valera and the Ulster Question,* p. 33. Iris Dháil Éireann, *Debate on the Treaty,* p. 157.

[29] 'The Devil's Carnival' in *The Collected Satires of Lord Alfred Douglas* (London, 1927). Alison Phillips, *The Revolution in Ireland,* pp. 236–37.

[30] Iris Dháil Éireann, *Debate on the Treaty,* pp. 329, 346–47.

Notes to Chapter 4

[1] Professor T.P. O'Neill argues that this is evidence of his 'inability as an actor': 'He had a ready-made opening line—"As I was saying when I was interrupted" but he muffed it. He could not pretend a spontaneity which was unreal. In fact he killed the line. He started off with a tribute to a previous speaker and followed it with a rather ponderous, "I am afraid . . ." . . .' (Foreword to Browne, *de Valera and the Banner County,* p. 11). To me it is evidence of very sophisticated acting: the great man gives the memorable line, well clothed with paraphernalia which emphasized his sincerity, his academic deliberation and his priestly superiority to the normal crudity of political jokes. And the line is delivered sufficiently late to ensure it is not drowned by any exultations at the opening.

[2] Longford and O'Neill, *de Valera,* p. 242. This portion of the speech is not included in Moynihan, *Speeches by de Valera,* p. 126. It represents the kind of historical retreat much used by de Valera when unsure of his ground.

[3] Moynihan, *Speeches by de Valera,* pp. 148–49. Since his release his followers had been forbidden to mention war at all, which was both natural to him and constructive within its limits (Longford and O'Neill, *de Valera,* p. 236).

[4] Professor J.J. Lee points out to me that the 'break with Sinn Féin was not on entering the Dáil, but on whether a decision to enter the Dáil could be classified as one of tactics rather than principle (a delicious Dev issue!)'. Principle, for Republicans, excluded any entry, tactics might permit it if principle were not in question.

[5] Murphy, 'The Achievement of Éamon de Valera', in Murphy and O'Connor, *De Valera and his Times,* p. 3.

6   Longford and O'Neill, *de Valera,* pp. 292–94.

7   Murphy, 'Achievement of de Valera', p. 7.

8   Robert Briscoe, with Alden Hatch, *For the Life of Me* (London, 1959), pp. 230–31.

9   Lee, 'Aspects of Corporatist Thought in Ireland: The Commission on Vocational Organisation, 1939–43', in Cosgrove and McCartney, eds., *Studies in Irish History Presented to R. Dudley Edwards,* pp. 324, 326, 328.

10   Iris Dháil Éireann, *Debate on the Treaty,* p. 274.

11   Dudley Edwards, 'Church and State in Modern Ireland', in Kevin B. Nowlan and T. Desmond Williams eds., *Ireland in the War Years and After 1939–51* (Dublin, 1969), p. 118.

12   Brian Farrell, *Seán Lemass* (Dublin, 1983), p. 45.

13   Ronan Fanning, 'Fianna Fáil and the Bishops', *Irish Times,* 13 and 14 February 1985. I am most grateful to Professor Brian Farrell for drawing to my attention, and sending me copies of, these important articles based on recently-opened Irish state archives. My interpretation of the documents differs slightly from that of Professor Fanning.

14   Moynihan, *Speeches by de Valera,* p. 580.

15   Lee, 'Continuity and Change in Ireland, 1945–70', in Lee ed., *Ireland 1945–70* (Dublin, 1979), pp. 169–70.

16   Quoted in Brian Farrell, *Chairman or Chief? The role of Taoiseach in Irish Government* (Dublin, 1971), p. 29. I have drawn deeply on the Cosgrave and de Valera sections of this brilliant analysis (pp. 1–42, 62–68).

17   Cruise O'Brien, 'The Embers of Easter', in Dudley Edwards and Pyle, *1916,* p. 232. 'There are things in this article—written in 1966—with which I am no longer in sympathy' (Cruise O'Brien, *States of Ireland,* p. 264); but I do not think the author repudiates this point.

18   Quoted in Deirdre McMahon, *Republicans and Imperialists: Anglo-Irish Relations in the 1930s* (New Haven, Conn., 1984), p. 101. I have learned much from this remarkable study based on archival evidence, but do not agree with its ascription to de Valera of 'refined intellectual thuggery' in prolonging cabinet meetings (p. 105).

19   Robert Fisk, *In Time of War: Ireland, Ulster and the Price of Neutrality 1939–45* (London, 1983), is valuable on Aiken as well as on de Valera in the war. On de Valera's wartime neutrality, Aiken would have been less an influence than a reminder of anti-British sentiment surviving among anti-Treaty Republicans. The wartime censorship under his aegis even purged favourable references to Jews from literary magazines, revealing a cast of mind quite alien from the pro-Jewish de Valera.

20   Liam C. Skinner, *Politicians by Accident* (Dublin, 1946), provides useful, if hagiographical, sketches of the de Valera cabinet; it tends to be overlooked, perhaps because the author later became chief political reporter for the hostile *Sunday Independent.*

21   Moynihan, *Speeches by de Valera,* pp. 323, 325–26, 335 and n. Dr Moynihan most honourably includes this excerpt from Mrs Clarke's speech.

22   P.S. O'Hegarty, *The Victory of Sinn Féin,* pp. 103–08, is peculiarly venomous about the women because so many were prominent against the Treaty. They are ably defended by Brian Farrell, 'Markievicz and the Women of the

Revolution', in Martin, *Leaders and Men,* pp. 227–38. Margaret Ward, *Unmanageable Revolutionaries—Women and Irish nationalism* (London, 1983), is assertively but somewhat mechanically feminist, culminating in an apparent tribute to Catherine Wheelwright at the expense of Sinéad (p. 287, n. 71). The betrayal of Irish feminism demands deeper study without its continued imprisonment in arid republicanism.

23 Gallagher, typescript 'De Valera', quoted in Bowman, *De Valera and the Ulster Question,* p. 330. See also pp. 78–79.

24 In his hilarious novel about Ireland in the Second World War, *The Elephant and the Kangaroo,* last two chapters. The speech there ascribed to de Valera is an exquisite caricature of his *pater patriae* style.

25 Joe Joyce and Peter Murtagh, *The Boss—Charles J. Haughey in Government* (Dublin, 1983), pp. 102–03.

26 p. 1.

27 Moynihan, *Speeches by de Valera,* pp. 474–75.

Epilogue by Rudyard Kipling

A St Helena Lullaby

How far is St Helena from a little child at play?
    What makes you want to wander there with all the world between?
Oh, Mother, call your son again or else he'll run away.
    (*No one thinks of winter when the grass is green!*)

How far is St Helena from a fight in Paris street?
    I haven't time to answer now—the men are falling fast.
The guns begin to thunder, and the drums begin to beat.
    (*If you take the first step you will take the last!*)

How far is St Helena from the field of Austerlitz?
    You couldn't hear me if I told—so loud the cannons roar.
But not so far for people who are living by their wits.
    (*'Gay go up' means 'gay go down' the wide world o'er!*)

How far is St Helena from an Emperor of France?
    I cannot see—I cannot tell— the crowns they dazzle so.
The Kings sit down to dinner, and the Queens stand up to dance.
    (*After open weather you may look for snow!*)

How far is St Helena from the Capes of Trafalgar?
    A longish way—a longish way—with ten year more to run.
It's South across the water underneath a setting star.
    (*What you cannot finish you must leave undone!*)

How far is St Helena from the Beresina ice?
    An ill way—a chill way—the ice begins to crack.
But not so far for gentlemen who never took advice.
    (*When you can't go forward you must e'en come back!*)

How far is St Helena from the field of Waterloo?
    A near way—a clear way— the ship will take you soon.
A pleasant place for gentlemen with little left to do.
    (*Morning never tries you till the afternoon!*)

How far from St Helena to the Gate of Heaven's Grace?
    That no one knows—that no one knows—and no one ever will.
But fold your hands across your heart and cover up your face,
    And after all your trapesings, child, lie still!

A Note on Sources

A biographer's needs are not always those of all students of history; a biographer whose childhood in a small country has overlapped with the later public life of his subject will have some needs that differ from those of the outsider. For instance, de Valera in his preface to Dorothy Macardle's *The Irish Republic* (London, 1937; also issued by the Left Book Club), said it "is an exhaustive chronicle of fact and provides the basis for an independent study of the period and considered judgement on it" which certainly makes it an important compendium of a version of events pleasing to him, but it was of little use to me. Its interpretation I knew from childhood reading of his newspapers the *Irish Press* and the *Sunday Press* in the 1940s and 1950s, and its selectivity made it most unhelpful on important points of detail. It reflected de Valera historiography at its apogee, which had its Stalinist flavour in ignoring as much as possible the conduct of those who at some time apostatized from him, and they were numerous.

But some publication from de Valera's apologists has been invaluable. Maurice Moynihan's edition of *Speeches and Statements by Éamon de Valera 1917–1973* (Dublin and New York, 1980) is a goldmine, and its detailed chronology a true friend for the biographer; in love and in scholarship, it is a work of great integrity. Thomas P. O'Neill's biography of de Valera is in Irish (with Pádraig Ó Fiannachta), in two volumes (Dublin, 1970), ending in 1937, and in English (with the Earl of Longford), in one (London, 1970), ending in 1970. The Irish version is much richer in documentary material, but the English has some interesting family reminiscence not in the Irish. It is its subject's version of events, sometimes wilful and sometimes not in its distortions, but Professor O'Neill went to much trouble to assist future historians who have been less grateful than they should have been. Seán P. Farragher, CSSP, *Dev and his Alma Mater* (Dublin, 1984), goes far beyond its subject and teems with documentary material on the early years. My obligations to it are immense. Mary Bromage, *De Valera and the March of a Nation* (Dublin, 1956), contains important detail obtained from interviews which cannot be found elsewhere.

Of other biographies, T. Ryle Dwyer has contributed three works, *Eamon de Valera* (Dublin, 1980), whence I derived little, *De Valera's Darkest Hour 1919–1932* and *De Valera's Finest Hour 1932–1959* (Cork, 1982), both of which I saw only after this book was in draft. I agree with him on de Valera's Wilsonian outlook, disagree on the success of the American mission, and salute the breadth of his researches. Denis Gwynn, *De Valera* (London, 1933), has some useful minor contemporary detail from a narrow hostile Redmondite outlook; Seán Ó Faoláin, *Life Story of Eamon de Valera* (Dublin, 1933) was later repudiated by its author and conveys, all too well, its subject's hagiographical appeal in 1932 for some young nationalist intellectuals, but his *De Valera* (London, 1939) has insights, weakened and strengthened by disillusion; Desmond Ryan, *Unique Dictator* (London, 1936), shows the attractiveness of de Valera to Irish exiles in Britain, and is important as the work of a Socialist pro-Treaty intellectual exceptional above humankind in his nobility; M.J. MacManus, *Eamon de Valera* (Dublin, 1944), is a dreadful revelation of the abysmally low level of intelligence ascribed to the party faithful to whom it is addressed. *De Valera and his Times* edited by John P. O'Carroll and John A. Murphy (Cork, 1983) is of mixed value, but its best work is very fine indeed: I derived most from the essays by Murphy, Farrell, Ó Tuathaigh, Fitzpatrick and Keogh. John Bowman is disappointing here on the earlier biographers, but his *De Valera and the Ulster Question 1917–1973* while a little narrowly political is rich in cool analysis and excellent quotation. Joseph Lee and M.A.G. Ó Tuathaigh, *The Age of de Valera* (Dublin, 1983), is fine, cool summary and analysis.

Apart from works listed in the footnotes, the following were also useful. Desmond Ryan, *Remembering Sion* (1934); Seán O'Casey, *Drums Under the Windows* (1945); Seán MacEntee, *Episode at Easter* (1966); Seán Cronin ed., *The McGarrity Papers* (1972); Robert Brennan, *Allegiance* (1950); Francis M. Carroll, *American Opinion and the Irish Question 1910–23* (1978); James Carty ed., *Bibliography of Irish History 1911–21;* Margery Forester, *Michael Collins* (1971); León Ó Broin, *Michael Collins* (1980); Calton Younger, *Ireland's Civil War* (1968); Edgar Holt, *Protest in Arms: The Irish Troubles 1916–23* (1961); R.B. McDowell, *The Irish*

Convention 1917–18 (1970); Brian Farrell, *The Founding of Dáil Éireann* (1971); Brian Farrell ed., *The Irish Parliamentary Tradition* (1973); Oliver MacDonagh, *Ireland* (1977) and *States of Mind* (1983); Frank Pakenham (later Earl of Longford) *Peace by Ordeal* (1935); Piaras Beaslái, *Michael Collins* (1926); Terence Brown, *Ireland: a Social and Cultural History 1922–79* (1981); Ronan Fanning, *Independent Ireland* (1983); Conor Cruise O'Brien ed., *The Shaping of Modern Ireland* (1960); Owen Dudley Edwards ed., *Conor Cruise O'Brien Introduces Ireland* (1969) (especially Cruise O'Brien, 'Ireland in International Affairs'); Francis MacManus ed., *The Years of the Great Test 1926–39* (1967); D.W. Harkness, *The Restless Dominion* (1969); Maurice Manning, *The Blueshirts* (1970); Peadar O'Donnell, *The Gates Flew open* (1966); J.H. Whyte, *Church and State in Modern Ireland 1923–1979* (1980); Maurice Manning, *Irish Political Parties* (1972); J.L. McCracken, *Representative Government in Ireland 1919–48* (1958); Seán O'Faolain, *The Irish* (1947, 1969, 1980); J.J. Lee ed., *Irish Historiography 1970–79* (1981); Kenneth O. Morgan, *Consensus and Disunity: The Lloyd George Coalition Government 1918–1922* (1979); A.J.P. Taylor, *English History 1914–1945* (1965); Tim Pat Coogan, *Ireland Since the Rising* (1966) and *The I.R.A.* (1970); J. Bowyer Bell, *The Secret Army* (1970); *Memoirs* of Desmond FitzGerald (1966); Joseph Carroll, *Ireland in the War Years 1939–45* (1975); Anne M. Brady and Brian Cleeve, *A Biographical Dictionary of Irish Writers* (1985); Henry Boylan, *A Dictionary of Irish Biography* (1978) (especially for Sinéad de Valera); the poems of W.B. Yeats, Thomas MacDonagh and John F. (Seán) MacEntee; G. Bernard Shaw, *The Matter with Ireland* (eds. Dan H. Laurence and David H. Greene; 1962); Francois Mauriac, *De Gaulle* (1964); and the Irish material in the periodical *The Round Table*.

The Author

Owen Dudley Edwards is unaware of any Welsh ancestors, but his mother was studying Welsh when he was born in Dublin in 1938. He was educated at Belvedere College and University College Dublin, some years after James Joyce. He studied at the Johns Hopkins University 1959–63, and has taught at the Universities of Oregon, Aberdeen, South Carolina, and California State at San Francisco. He is Reader in Commonwealth and American History at the University of Edinburgh, which he joined in 1968.

His wife is American, his three children are Scots, his books include *Celtic Nationalism* (with Gwynfor Evans, Ioan Rees and Hugh MacDiarmid), as well as studies of James Connolly, Arthur Conan Doyle, P.G. Wodehouse, and Thomas Babington Macaulay (to be published in 1988). He is a Roman Catholic and a member of Plaid Cymru.

The General Editor

Kenneth O. Morgan F.B.A., D.Litt., is Fellow and Praelector of The Queen's College, Oxford. Born in Middlesex of north Cardiganshire and Meirionethshire origins he is an eminent historian and prolific author. He has written extensively and authoritatively on Radical movements in nineteenth-century and early twentieth-century Britain; his titles include *Wales in British Politics 1868–1922* (1963), *David Lloyd George* (1963), *Keir Hardie* (1975), *Rebirth of a Nation: Wales 1880–1980* (1981) and *Labour in Power 1945–1951* (1984). He has been editor of *The Welsh History Review* since 1965 and was elected a Fellow of the British Academy in 1983.